The Promise of the Holy Spirit

You Were Meant for Something More

PAUL BALIUS

HA'KODESH PUBLISHING

The Promise of the Holy Spirit

Published by HA'KODESH PUBLISHING

ISBN 978-1-7349097-0-8 (paperback)
ISBN 978-1-7349097-1-5 (epub)

Cover and interior illustration of dove by Ilse Kleyn, *artofkleyn.com*

Interior illustration of child praying, Sketches by Paul, *Sketchesbypaul.wordpress.com*

Other imagery by *Adobestock.com*

Editorial services by Thomas Womack, *BookOx.com*

Proofreading by Dana L. Cobb

Design by Monica Thomas for TLC Book Design, *TLCBookDesign.com*

The John Wesley account in chapter 22 is taken from *E. M. Bounds on Prayer* (New Kensington, Pennsylvania: Whitaker House, 1997), 270.

PRINTED IN THE UNITED STATES OF AMERICA

Contents

(Contents continued)

INTRODUCTION

You Were Meant for Something More

We cannot reach the end of the possibilities God has for us. There's a height we can never get to, because it goes on forever. Yet we can grow nearer every day.

I don't know where you are with your faith, but I know we're all still growing. Perhaps you think you've reached some limit. Or perhaps you long for something greater but you aren't gaining ground. Child of God, He has more for you, if you would simply press into it.

Wherever you are in your faith journey, God wants to take you higher. *You were meant for something more.*

I used to think I couldn't make it higher in my faith. It seemed that no matter how hard I tried, my faith grew only in knowledge and not in power. For many years I studied everything I could about the things of the Lord. I studied the Bible and was immersed in it day and night. I listened to the most brilliant Christian speakers of our day. I read books from some of the most anointed teachers throughout history. I was walking in greater knowledge, but not in greater power. Knowledge knows what to do, but it takes power to actually do it.

For fourteen years, I served in various capacities in prison ministry. When I started teaching and preaching in prisons about the power of God, I hadn't yet walked in this power. My preaching was more theory than practice. I wanted more than I had, but I had no idea how I might get there.

Then everything changed.

Child of God, my hope and prayer is that you will also be able to say this about your life with the Holy Spirit: "Then everything changed."

You can walk in the power of the Holy Spirit so that your life will never be the same. God can do such a mighty work in you that you won't even recognize the person who looks back at you in the mirror each morning.

My desire is not to impress you with what the Lord has done for me, but rather what He can do for you. There's so much more for you. God has ordained for you a life you cannot imagine. Child of God, you were meant for something more!

Child of God, you were meant for something more!

Sometimes we read of what others have attained spiritually and we think they attained this by their own ability. We consider our own weaknesses and believe that we cannot obtain what others have been able to take hold of. Child of God, rebuke that thought right now in the name of Jesus. You will be changed not by your abilities, but by His. God isn't limited in what He can do for any of us, except when we refuse to let Him. Let God have His way in your life.

About twenty years ago, I had the privilege of being called by God to write. After this calling, I was reading *Loving God* by Chuck Colson. In one of the chapters, I read about a retired woman in a nursing home who wrote to prisoners. I felt the leading of the Lord that this would be the first way in which I would write for the kingdom. Let the Lord do the calling—then be obedient to whatever He would have you do.

I served in the ministry founded by Chuck Colson called Prison Fellowship Ministries. For seven years, I wrote and ministered to several prisoners located across the country. This writing was a ministry done alone in my room at home, without any applause or attention. How much we need to learn to serve in obscurity. I would handwrite each letter, and I got to know many men and all that they were going through.

After these seven years, I was called by the Lord to serve inside prisons. I became part of a ministry that was also with Prison Fellowship Ministries. I joined this ministry program, where I served in three different prisons for the next seven years.

While I was serving inside these prisons, my faith was increased dramatically. I met so many anointed men and women of God who poured spiritual blessings into my life. I began to walk in the gifts of the Holy Spirit. I began to hear the whispers of the Holy Spirit every day. I began to write in a daily devotion all that I heard from the Holy Spirit, a practice that I've continued for many years.

Most often, I hear from the Lord about what I need to learn at that point in my life. We're all on a journey. You may wonder if God still speaks to this day. Child of God, the Lord has never lost His voice, and He never will.

Eventually the Lord called me out of the prison ministry and placed me where I could begin to write more intensely.

God had spent fourteen years doing a work *in* me before He had me where He could then do this new work *through* me. We must never rush the Lord in His plans for us, but simply serve faithfully as He prepares us for all that He would have us do. You don't have to be in a hurry when you're saved for all eternity.

And so, my writing ministry began. I've been writing with an intensity and a passion to help others grow in their spiritual life. It's not enough that our faith is stirred up; we must also stir up others.

My prayer is to see God's children grow in His calling on their life, that they would radically increase in their faith and take hold of the promises stored up in His Word.

You were meant for something more, and the something more is nothing less than being filled with the Spirit of God.

His calling isn't dependent on you, but is rooted in Himself, that you would live out all that He has ordained for you to become. Be sure that God has a purpose for you, then be ready to let Him prepare you for all that He would have you do. You were meant for something more, and the something more is nothing less than being filled with the Spirit of God.

Everything I write is the culmination of listening intently to the Holy Spirit every day over a period of many years. I find that sometimes it can take me an hour to hear a single word from the Holy Spirit. Sometimes that means fifty-nine minutes of striving for it, and finally one minute of surrendering to Him in which I can then hear the word. The key is whether we'll wait that fifty-nine minutes trusting that He will give us a word.

Dare to trust God. My greatest desire is that God's children would all hear the Holy Spirit in their lives.

The writing style I use is to offer a narrative or a short teaching about a topic. Then I will include words on that particular topic that I've heard from the Holy Spirit over the last several years. These words I've heard from the Holy Spirit are shown in *italics*.

Always discern for yourself what is right as you read words from me or anyone else. Only God is infallible; the rest of us are not. Use the plumb line of truth found only in the Word of God. At the same time, put down the blinders of man's traditions and the limits placed on God by many in our day.

My worry in our day is that many are rejecting the Holy Spirit just as they rejected Jesus when He came to earth. The elite in the day of Jesus were so wrapped up in their interpretation of Scripture that they couldn't see the Scriptures revealed in the One standing before them. In our day we also have the manifestation of God on earth—no longer in His Son Jesus, but now with the Holy Spirit. And some today will argue away the power and the gifts of the Holy Spirit, just as some argued away the power and the gifts that flowed through Jesus in His day. Child of God, don't reject the Holy Spirit, but welcome Him as your Friend.

Beware of the arguments of man that would limit the power of God we're meant to have in this day. We're meant to have the Holy Spirit working mightily in us and through us, by which we can then reach a dark and dying world around us. There are people around you depending upon you to be the one who will dare to be used of God and filled with the Holy Spirit. Dare to believe God. Be that one. You were meant for something more and it is up to you to step into it.

Pray to the Father and to the Lord Jesus Christ that the Holy Spirit would guide you and teach you in all things. With the Holy Spirit as our Teacher, there's no limit to what we might learn. With the Holy Spirit in us, there is no limit to what God might do through us.

With the Holy Spirit as our Teacher, there's no limit to what we might learn.

Many of the Scripture quotations on these pages are from the *New King James Version* which was the standard version we used in prison ministry. Please look up the verses in the translation you prefer to use. The best translation is the one you read. An even better translation is the one you live.

Blessings to you,
Paul

1 The Promise of the Holy Spirit

There is nothing impossible for God—not even you.

It was always God's plan to place His own Spirit in us, such that we could live a life not possible in any other way. The Father promised us, "I will put My Spirit within you" (Ezekiel 36:27).

There are more promises in the Word of God than we've yet taken hold of. When the Father makes a promise, He'll always keep it. God is faithful. God cannot fail. But it's up to us to believe and then to receive His promises. "Having believed, you were sealed with the Holy Spirit of promise" (Ephesians 1:13).

The prophetic promise of the Holy Spirit being poured into us was given many times throughout the Word of God. These prophecies came from the Father through the kings, the priests, the prophets, and finally by the Son of God Himself in Christ Jesus.

The Father told the prophet Isaiah that the blessings were coming with the Holy Spirit: “I will pour out my Spirit on your descendants, and my blessing on your children” (Isaiah 44:3 NLT).

Moses expressed his desire for a greater outpouring of the Holy Spirit: “Oh, that all the LORD’s people were prophets and that the LORD would put His Spirit upon them!” (Numbers 11:29).

The Lord gave the prophet Ezekiel these prophetic words: “I will put My Spirit in you” (Ezekiel 37:14).

We drink when we’re thirsty. Do you thirst to have an outpouring of the Holy Spirit upon you? Do you long to be empowered by the Holy Spirit to live a life you could live by no other means? Pray for it. If we lack the promises of God in our life, this is never because His promises are lacking, but because we aren’t pressing in to receive them. Ask for the Holy Spirit with a child-like faith. *Don’t be such a grown-up that you’re no longer a child of God.*

Don’t be such a grown-up that you’re no longer a child of God.

Through the prophet Joel, the Father promised the outpouring of the Holy Spirit: “I will pour out my Spirit upon all people. Your sons and daughters will prophesy. Your old men will dream dreams, and your young men will see visions” (Joel 2:28 NLT).

John the Baptist prophesied the coming baptism of the Holy Spirit through Jesus Christ: “I indeed baptized you with water, but He [Jesus] will baptize you with the Holy Spirit” (Mark 1:8).

Jesus received the promise of the Holy Spirit first, as Peter explained on the day of Pentecost: “Having received from the Father the promise of the Holy Spirit, He [Jesus] poured out this [manifestation of the Holy Spirit] which you now see and hear” (Acts 2:33).

Jesus promised before His death that we would receive the Holy Spirit: "But the Helper, the Holy Spirit, whom the Father will send in My name, He will teach you all things, and bring to your remembrance all things that I said to you" (John 14:26).

When Jesus was raised from death back to life, He reaffirmed the promise from the Father about the Holy Spirit: "And being assembled together with them, He commanded them not to depart from Jerusalem, but to wait for the Promise of the Father, 'which,' He said, 'you have heard from Me'" (Acts 1:4).

Man will promise you the world yet always leave you wanting. The Father never breaks a promise, but we must receive the promise to realize it in our life. Never stop pressing in for the Spirit-filled life. Jesus didn't come to only save us and then leave us to live some meager, half-baked Christian life. No, He promised us that the Father would send the Holy Spirit, the Helper, to help us.

We're needy creatures desperately in need of the Holy Spirit. Wherever you're flatlining or failing in your life, you're living apart from the power of the Holy Spirit within you.

We now live in the day in which the prophecy can be fulfilled and we can receive the Holy Spirit: "Then they laid hands on them, and they received the Holy Spirit" (Acts 8:17).

The Holy Spirit does not come by our effort but by our surrender. We cannot earn the Holy Spirit, but only humbly receive Him as a gift from the Father. "You shall receive the gift of the Holy Spirit" (Acts 2:38).

The Holy Spirit will lead us, but it is up to us to follow Him. "For all who are allowing themselves to be led by the Spirit of God are sons of God" (Romans 8:14 AMP).

God knew we could never make it on our own, and that's why His prophecies

We cannot earn the Holy Spirit, but only humbly receive Him as a gift from the Father.

pointed to having His Spirit in us. He can do in us by His Spirit what we could never do on our own.

Stop agonizing over your lack of strength, and pray that He would fill you with His strength. The hindrance to *His* work in us is *our* work in us. You must kneel to grow higher, and you must bow down to be lifted up.

God made you; be sure that He can change you. "I will put my Spirit inside you and cause you to live by my laws, respect my rulings and obey them" (Ezekiel 36:27 CJB).

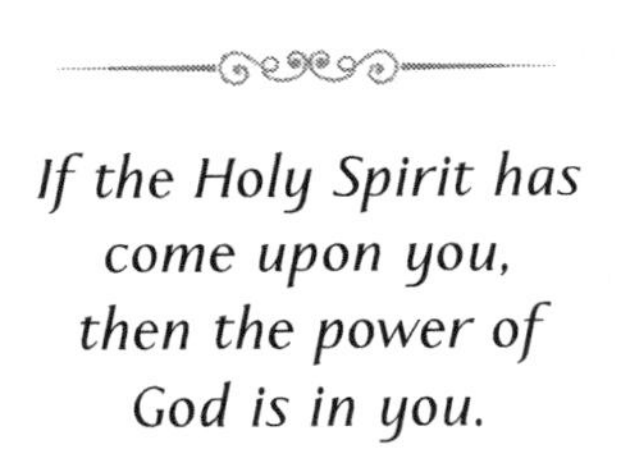
If the Holy Spirit has
come upon you,
then the power of
God is in you.

If the Holy Spirit has come upon you, then the power of God is in you. Jesus promised, "You shall receive power when the Holy Spirit has come upon you" (Acts 1:8).

Don't just get filled once with the Holy Spirit, but keep getting filled. Our natural bodies leak, and our natural surroundings dry us up. Every day we must pray that the Father would pour out His Holy Spirit upon us. If you want more, ask for more. Jesus taught us, "How much more will your heavenly Father give the Holy Spirit to those who ask Him!" (Luke 11:13).

I used to wonder why Jesus would make such outrageous demands that we live holy lives, since He knows we're such weak creatures. Jesus commands us, "Therefore you shall be perfect, just as your Father in heaven is perfect" (Matthew 5:48). Jesus knows we couldn't do this in our flesh, but only by the Holy Spirit of God reigning in us. Jesus knew that the Father would send the Holy Spirit to give us power to live a holy life.

Jesus came to shed His blood to cover our sin. The Holy Spirit came to give us power and victory over sin. It's up to us to receive from Jesus our salvation and then to receive from the Holy Spirit the power to get the victory. The Father promised us a new life by

His Spirit, but we must receive it by faith— "that we might receive the promise of the Spirit through faith" (Galatians 3:14).

The promise of the Holy Spirit is for all those who are the called of God. In Peter's message after receiving the Holy Spirit at Pentecost, he proclaimed, "You shall receive the gift of the Holy Spirit. For the promise is to you and to your children, and to all who are afar off, as many as the Lord our God will call" (Acts 2:38-39). The promises of God are stronger than the failures of man.

The promises of God are stronger than the failures of man.

The promise of the Holy Spirit is the promise of the Father to give us everything we need to live a life pleasing to Himself. When we have the Spirit of God reigning within us, there's nothing we will lack in being able to live a godly life. God can do in us what we could never do on our own.

There is no such thing as a self-made saint. "We are being transfigured into His very image as we move from one brighter level of glory to another. And this glorious transfiguration comes from the Lord, who is the [Holy] Spirit" (2 Corinthians 3:18 TPT).

There are some things that only the Holy Spirit can teach you. "These things we also speak, not in words which man's wisdom teaches but which the Holy Spirit teaches" (1 Corinthians 2:13).

On our own, we could never be perfect. But when we yield ourselves to the power of the Holy Spirit living inside us, He can be perfect through us. When we realize the power of the Holy Spirit and we yield to Him, then the words of Christ no longer seem impossible. We can live in a newness of life because the new life is the Holy Spirit living within us.

Beloved child of God, you were meant for something more. The something more is nothing less than the Spirit of God living inside you. Nothing is impossible for God when once you yield to Him.

Take hold of the promise of the Holy Spirit in your life. "...take hold of the gift of the Holy Spirit" (Acts 2:38 TPT).

A Prayer for Understanding the Promise of the Holy Spirit in Our Life

Below and near the end of each chapter in this book, you'll find a prayer to each Person of the Trinity—the Father, the Son, and the Holy Spirit. Some say we can pray only to the Father. Some will add that we can pray to Jesus. Others will also pray to the Holy Spirit, as I do. My prayers are different for each distinct Person of the Trinity. All three in the Trinity are one God, yet three distinct Persons. The Father is God, Jesus is God, and the Holy Spirit is God. When we pray to God, we pray to all three. When we pray to any one of the three, we pray to God.

* *Father God, show me in Your Word the truth and the promise of Your plan to fill me with Your Spirit. Help me to receive the promise and the power of the Holy Spirit dwelling within me.*

* *Lord Jesus, thank you for dying on the cross to pay for my sins so that I could live forever with You. Thank You for promising that the Holy Spirit would come to help me and teach me forever.*

* *Holy Spirit, I pray that You would convict me into the will of the Father and the heart of Jesus Christ. Lead me so that I please the Father and the Son in everything I say and do.*

Spiritual Guide

Each chapter in this book ends with three things you should do in your spiritual journey. Some of these you may already have done, but I would encourage you to prayerfully consider what more God would have you do in each one of them. Faith is like a tree that's meant to grow and to continue producing fruit. Ask God to help you. Let God help you. Always seek to be pliable in the hands of God.

- If you haven't turned from your life of sin and surrendered your life over to Jesus Christ, do that today. It doesn't matter how far you are from God, but only that you've turned away from evil to go toward Him. Until you give your life to Jesus, the Holy Spirit will not come upon you. As the apostle Peter preached, "Repent [turn] and return to God, and each one of you must be baptized in the name of Jesus, the Anointed One, to have your sins removed. Then you may take hold of the gift of the Holy Spirit" (Acts 2:38 TPT).

- If you don't pray every day, start doing that today. Pray when you wake up, pray just before you go to bed, and then over time, start praying in between those two times, until prayer becomes your life. "Rejoice always, pray without ceasing, in everything give thanks; for this is the will of God in Christ Jesus for you" (1 Thessalonians 5:16-18).

- If you aren't reading the Word of God every day, start doing that today. You must get into the Word for the Word to be in you. Don't try to read too much at once; let it work on you a little at a time. "Your word I have hidden in my heart, that I might not sin against You" (Psalm 119:11).

2 Being Filled with the Holy Spirit

You don't need a program—you need the Holy Spirit.

It is God's will that we should be filled with the Holy Spirit. "So then do not be foolish, but understand what the will of the Lord is.... Be filled with the Spirit" (Ephesians 5:17–18 NASB).

Child of God, this filling of the Holy Spirit is for you. This life isn't reserved for the special few; it's available to all who will dare to live the life filled with the Spirit of God. God's promise was to pour out His Spirit over all of us. "I will pour out my Spirit upon all people" (Joel 2:28 NLT).

I want you to know that however you might be lacking in the fullness of the Holy Spirit right now, the Lord still waits to fill you. Keep pressing in. Keep desiring more. There are no limits to what

God can do. Stop thinking *you* must do something when it's God who does all the work. All you have to do is let Him.

There are no limits to being filled with the Holy Spirit. Scarcity is a word not found in the dictionary of heaven. You can receive to the degree that you let Him have His way in your life. The Spirit-filled life is made fuller when we empty out the natural life that consumes us. Being Spirit-filled is the heavenly life we can have right now. You don't have to wait until you're in heaven; you can have heaven fill you today.

Whatever fills you defines you.

The Holy Spirit in you changes you.

The Holy Spirit in you completes you.

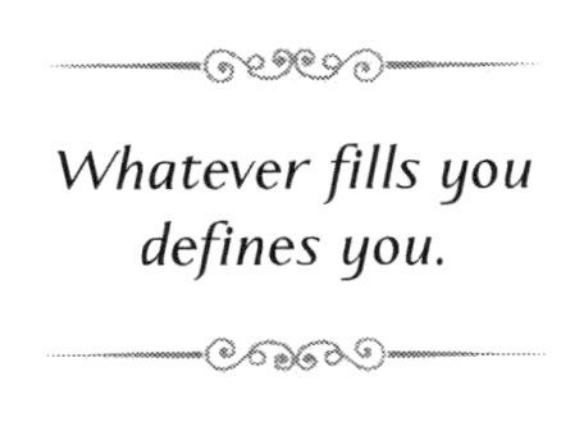
Whatever fills you defines you.

Perhaps you have a filling of the Holy Spirit already. I want to encourage you to press in for more. The Holy Spirit is like a river, always flowing, always moving. Our spiritual life isn't meant to be a destination but a journey. Keep growing. Keep pressing in for more. Keep allowing the Lord to have a greater reign in your life.

When you're filled with the Holy Spirit, you can sense the deep presence of the Holy Spirit dwelling in others. Sometimes I'll sense that someone across the room is filled with the Spirit of God. We'll look at each other, and even if we never say a word to one another, there's something divine in which we share.

This sensing of the Spirit in another is not for our promotion, but for the glory of God. When you receive the Holy Spirit in greater measure, you'll realize how much you don't deserve Him. It's only by the grace of God that we can have the Spirit of God dwelling within us. We don't deserve all the blessings that God pours out upon us, and we most certainly cannot take any credit for them.

Child of God, there's more to this Christian life than you can imagine. God's imagination is not limited by yours. He has plans for you that you've never dreamed of. To reach for the heavens requires that you be filled with power from God. You were meant to be filled with the Holy Spirit. The promises of God are necessary for the purposes of God to be fulfilled through you.

You were meant to be filled with the Holy Spirit.

To reach your potential, you need His Spirit to help you. There are some things you were never meant to do apart from God within you. There are people on this planet who need you to press in for everything God would do through you, so that you'll be a blessing to them. It's not about you, but God through you. Don't squander what God has for you.

To teach others the Spirit-filled life, see to it that they themselves become filled. "Then they began laying their hands on them, and they were receiving the Holy Spirit" (Acts 8:17 NASB).

You don't need natural talent, but spiritual power. You would not need so many gimmicks if you just had the Holy Spirit. "For our gospel did not come to you in word only, but also in power, and in the Holy Spirit" (1 Thessalonians 1:5).

If you want to change the world, first let the Holy Spirit change you. "We are being changed into His image with ever-increasing glory. This comes from the Lord, who is the Spirit" (2 Corinthians 3:18 NOG).

Nobody is filled by a fraction of the Holy Spirit, but by the fullness of God. "Be filled with all the fullness of God" (Ephesians 3:19).

Nobody is filled by a fraction of the Holy Spirit, but by the fullness of God.

Trying to explain the Spirit-filled life is like trying to explain falling in love. Thousands of love poems have been written, and thousands more love songs, but it's not until a person actually falls in love that they can truly understand. The same is true with being filled with the Holy Spirit. Still, we must try, we must encourage, we must teach on all that the Holy Spirit can do in the life of a believer who actually believes.

The same Holy Spirit that filled the apostles fills you. Stop thinking God cannot do great things through you. It's not about you.

The proof of the Holy Spirit in you is what flows out from you. The waters are not still, but flowing. The Lord Jesus said, "He who believes in Me, as the Scripture has said, out of his heart will flow rivers of living water" (John 7:38).

We don't need a new way, but to return to the old. To solve today's problems, we need the same Holy Spirit power that the first-century church had. "And they chose Stephen, a man full of faith and the Holy Spirit.... And Stephen, full of faith and power, did great wonders and signs among the people" (Acts 6:5,8). Imagine a church with even a few believers filled by the Holy Spirit. It always begins with that one believer. Be that one.

I was a Christian for many years before I was filled with the Holy Spirit. I saw people who had a deep filling of the Holy Spirit upon them, but I didn't know how to reach for it. I thought I could attain this deeper filling through study, but knowing about the Holy Spirit is something far different from being filled with the Holy Spirit.

As I progressed in my faith, I thought I had to be more productive—that by works I could earn the right to be filled with the Holy Spirit. I served more and more, trying with all my might to please the Lord, that He might grant to me a greater filling of His Spirit. But what I learned was that all my effort was in vain; it was actually the hindrance to all that God could do in me.

Child of God, there's only one way we'll find victory in the Lord, and that is in being surrendered to Him. It's only by our willing submission that the Holy Spirit is poured into us in greater measure. We must learn about humility, pray for humility, seek humility, and walk in humility, that we might then be found ready to be used of God. Much of our efforts are born out of pride, and pride stands as the barrier to what God can do in us.

Sacrifice your life to Him, and He will give His life to you.

Hindrances to Being Filled

You can't be filled with the Holy Spirit if you're full of yourself. "For those who identify with their old nature set their minds on the things of the old nature, but those who identify with the Spirit set their minds on the things of the Spirit" (Romans 8:5 CJB).

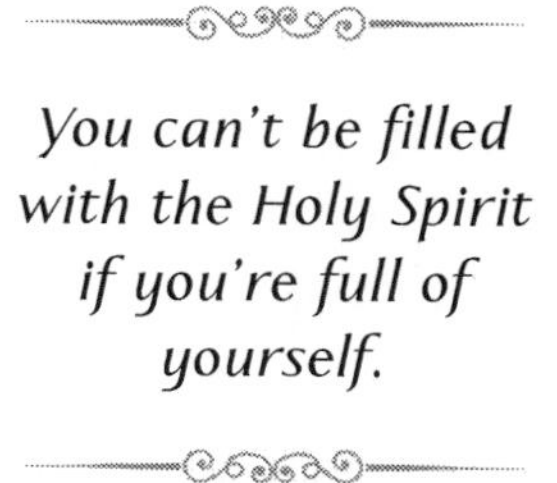
You can't be filled with the Holy Spirit if you're full of yourself.

Scripture tells us to be filled with the Spirit, and there is no emptying in the instructions that follow.

The ability of God to use you has more to do with your surrendering than His conquering.

Beware of organizing the spontaneity of the Holy Spirit right out of your life. "If we live in the Spirit, let us also walk in the Spirit" (Galatians 5:25).

The harder you try, the less you have. The more it's about you, the less it's about Him in you. The world says to be strong; God says to be weak. "For when I am weak, then I am strong" (2 Corinthians 12:10).

The ability of God to use you has more to do with your surrendering than His conquering.

The only man who can argue against the power of the Holy Spirit is the one who does not have the power.

The Holy Spirit cannot do a work through you until He has first done a work in you. The apostle Paul prayed, "that He would grant you, according to the riches of His glory, to be strengthened with might through His Spirit in the inner man" (Ephesians 3:16).

Keep Pressing In

Keep pressing in until you have from God what you cannot live without. Don't wait until you get to heaven for those things that

God can give you right now. Even if it takes you twenty years to get it, keep pressing in for it. I can tell you it took me years, but when it came it was all worth it.

Never give up until you take hold of all that God has for you.

Jesus promised, "You will receive power and ability when the Holy Spirit comes upon you" (Acts 1:8 AMP). *The proof of power is power.*

Keep asking until you receive all that the Lord has for you. "Ask, and the gift is yours.... For every persistent one will get what he asks for" (Matthew 7:7-8 TPT).

Sometimes God delays answering your requests to see just how serious you are about them.

Be patient with all that God would do for you. As you're waiting, He's preparing you for what He would have you do later. Never rush the eternal God who knows the best timing. Just believe and keep serving Him, so that in your serving He gives you everything you need.

I've found that in some things with the Lord I had to wait for years, and in others I didn't have to wait at all. You can be sure that God knows what He's doing all the time. Learn to trust His timing, but never stop asking for the promises He has given in His Word. I remind Him of what He has spoken in His Word. This is not to imply that He has forgotten His Word, but only to let Him know that I believe His Word and I'm standing on His promises.

A Prayer to Be Filled with the Holy Spirit

* *Father God, You promised that You would put Your Spirit inside me, and that by Your Spirit You would cause me to walk in Your ways. Father, I pray that You would do this for me more each day.*

* *Lord Jesus, just as the Holy Spirit came upon the apostles, the same Holy Spirit can come upon me. You promised that the Father would send the Holy Spirit. Help me to receive the fullness of the Holy Spirit.*

* *Holy Spirit, help me every day to keep pressing in until Your fullness is upon me. Help me to see that it's not by my qualifications that I am filled, but only by my willing submission to the Father.*

Spiritual Guide

* Give yourself grace in the journey that the Lord has you in. It's in the journey that the Lord is changing you. Just keep pressing in. "Create in me a clean heart, O God, and renew a steadfast spirit within me. Do not cast me away from Your presence, and do not take Your Holy Spirit from me" (Psalm 51:10-11).

* If you have a worldly jealousy for someone else, especially in ministry, confess it and rebuke it in the name of Jesus. Worldly jealousy is born out of the wrong spirit. We need to get things right with others if we're to get things right with God. "You are still worldly.... For as long as there is jealousy and strife

and discord among you, are you not unspiritual, and are you not walking like ordinary men [unchanged by faith]?" (1 Corinthians 3:3 AMP).

* In whatever prayer meeting or church you attend, seek to find the one in authority to whom you can submit to. When we submit to those God has placed in authority, we're revealing that we're submitted to God. "In the same way, you who are younger must accept the authority of the elders. And all of you, dress yourselves in humility as you relate to one another, for 'God opposes the proud but gives grace to the humble'" (1 Peter 5:5 NLT).

3 Surrendering to the Holy Spirit

The great struggle we have in the Christian faith is that we think it's a great struggle. It is not a great struggle; it's a great surrender.

It has always been God's plan that we would surrender ourselves to the Holy Spirit within us. "Or do you not know that your body is the temple of the Holy Spirit who is in you, whom you have from God, and you are not your own? For you were bought at a price; therefore glorify God in your body and in your spirit, which are God's" (1 Corinthians 6:19–20).

In my faith journey, I've experienced two main segments: first, when I was striving to be filled with the Holy Spirit, and second, when I surrendered to the Holy Spirit.

Many Christians are satisfied with very little. Some Christians desire and strive for something more, though they're unable to grasp it. It's the blessed few who discover that all they need to do is surrender themselves unto God to gain it all.

This surrendering isn't reserved for the few, but it's found by only the few. The reason so few have this surrendering in their life is not because it's so hard, but because it's so easy. In our old nature, we still have the pride that says we must do something in order that we might gain something. But it's the divine plan of God that we can do nothing of ourselves and must learn to throw ourselves utterly helpless before Him, that He would then reign in our lives.

In the world, to gain more you must be more. In the kingdom, to gain more you must be less. "The high and lofty one who lives in eternity, the Holy One, says this: 'I live in the high and holy place with those whose spirits are contrite and humble. I restore the crushed spirit of the humble and revive the courage of those with repentant hearts'" (Isaiah 57:15 NLT).

In the world, to gain more you must be more. In the kingdom, to gain more you must be less.

Man measures us by what we have. God measures us by what we surrender.

The higher calling is not a greater gaining but an absolute surrender. The Lord Jesus is not searching for part-time believers or two scoops of faith. Jesus taught, "And you shall love the Lord your God with all your heart, with all your soul, with all your mind, and with all your strength" (Mark 12:30).

Surrendering is the prerequisite to our being filled with the Holy Spirit. Being filled with the Holy Spirit is not an intellectual exercise but a determination of your will. Either you'll have it your way, or you'll let Him have His way in you. There's no halfway mark in the life of a man or woman completely surrendered to God. Give Him your everything, and He will be everything in you.

We have the false worldly idea that He expects us to do more before He will do more. The truth is that He'll do more when you realize and confess that you cannot do it.

Your first great deliverance is from the bondage of sin. Your second great deliverance is from the bondage of self. The first comes by the blood of Christ alone. The second comes by the power of the Holy Spirit alone. Both require the surrendering of yourself that you would receive the gift—first of salvation, then of sanctification.

The price of growing in the Spirit is nothing less than your right to yourself. This is why only the few walk in the Spirit, because many consider this price too high. If they would simply press in, they would find that the deal is far more unfair than they imagined—but the other way around. When we give our life to Jesus, He then gives the life of His Spirit to us. His life is so much greater than our own. If you want the Holy Spirit to reign in your life, *you* cannot reign in your life.

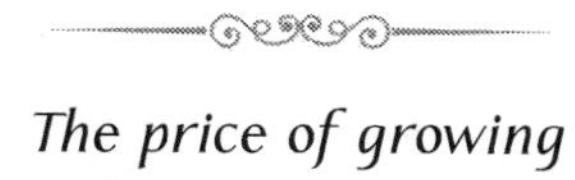

The price of growing in the Spirit is nothing less than your right to yourself.

If you want to be filled with the Holy Spirit, you cannot be full of yourself. You think you're holding on to something better, but it's a vapor that will amount to nothing. You're trading a moment and losing for all eternity. We don't have to wait until we're in heaven to be filled with God; we can do it right now, here on earth.

The prerequisite to being led by the Spirit is your willingness to follow Him. "For as many as are led by the Spirit of God, they are the sons of God" (Romans 8:14 KJV).

You need the Holy Spirit in you for the purposes of God to flow through you. "And neither the delivery nor the content of my message relied on compelling words of 'wisdom' but on a demonstration of the power of the Spirit" (1 Corinthians 2:4 CJB).

You need the Holy Spirit in you for the purposes of God to flow through you.

For Him to be strong in you, be weak. For Him to give over to you, give up. Do the opposite of what the world says to do, and you will be walking in kingdom principles.

One time I was at a service, and the atmosphere was flowing in the Spirit. I was on my feet and praying for a greater filling of the Holy Spirit. How much we all need to be continually seeking that greater filling, such that the power of God would come upon us more and more.

As I stood there at the service, I was so completely overwhelmed that I could no longer stand on my own power. My arms were stretched out to heaven, and I could feel the Spirit flowing down and intertwining with me and holding me up. It was as if I was being held up by spiritual strands from heaven that weaved throughout my body. I don't understand how everything from heaven works, but I know when I'm being touched by the things of heaven.

This isn't the norm in my life, and I worry that many chase these experiences more than they should. While I'm lifted by experiences such as these, my faith life with God is normally simple and mundane, from which little may be written, but by which my heart is rich because of the ever-present Spirit of God. While I love mountain-top experiences, I know the Lord has plans for me to accomplish His will down in the valley. The same is true for you. The mountain-top experiences prepare us, but the valley is where the work gets done.

The mountain-top experiences prepare us, but the valley is where the work gets done.

We imagine that the apostles had some special Holy Spirit, while we at best have a lesser ranking Holy Spirit. Child of God, there's only one Holy Spirit, the Spirit of God. If you only knew the power that was in you, you might barely be able to sleep at night.

The same Holy Spirit who dwelt in Peter dwells in you. "They even carried their sick out into the streets and put them on cots and sleeping pads, so that when Peter came by at least his shadow might fall on one of them [with healing power]" (Acts 5:15 AMP).

The struggle we have in growing spiritually is that we try to do so by natural means. But the less we strive, the more it will flow. This is because striving is in the natural, which is the obstacle to the spiritual.

For many years I'd been growing in my faith, deep in the Word, attending services, serving the Lord, and all the while longing for something more. It seemed that no matter how hard I tried, I was growing only in knowledge and not in the Spirit. Yet this was a season that had to precede the next. Never despair where you are; just keep pressing into where the Lord is taking you.

The Lord will never take you to level two until He has first accomplished everything He has intended to achieve in you at level one. Be content where you are, while at the same time always desiring something more. Learn to do the great work of resting in the Lord.

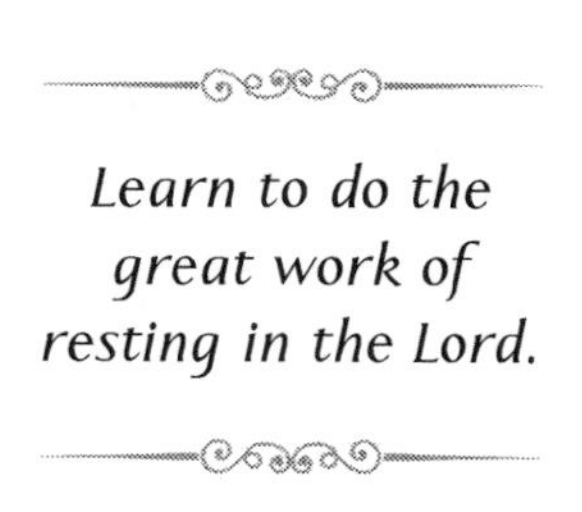
Learn to do the great work of resting in the Lord.

It wouldn't be so hard for you to move in the spiritual if you weren't trying so hard in your natural. "Someone living on an entirely human level rejects the revelations of God's Spirit, for they make no sense to him. He can't understand the revelations of the Spirit because they are only discovered by the illumination of the Spirit" (1 Corinthians 2:14 TPT).

You cannot grow in the Spirit unless the Holy Spirit reigns in you. If you are not growing, you can be sure that you are the problem in the equation between the Holy Spirit and you.

Finally, in my faith journey, I crossed into the precious secret of heaven for spiritual growth—that we don't have to do a thing except surrender. People try to make it more complicated or self-generated. There's nothing hard that a man or woman must do when it's the Lord who does the work. We're such prideful creatures in thinking that certainly we must do part of the work. We can do nothing but get in the way. Get out of His way.

The greatest deliverance for man is from himself. "Jesus said to all of his followers, 'If you truly desire to be My disciple, you must disown your life completely, embrace My 'cross' as your own, and surrender to My ways'" (Luke 9:23 TPT).

You cannot hear in the spiritual realm with natural ears, and so long as you try, you will only hinder His ability to speak to you. That is why the strongest people often gain the least in the heavenly realm, since they don't know how to be weak in the natural realm.

The more selfless you are, the more the Holy Spirit can fill you.

The more selfless you are, the more the Holy Spirit can fill you.

It's now my purpose on this earth to encourage and draw others into this precious and spiritually rich life that's soaked in the Spirit and held together by the power of God. I received this phrase from the Lord: "*Don't try to impress others with who you are, but inspire them with who they can become.*" Oh, child of God, you were meant for something more.

Our spiritual potential remains buried beneath anything of our natural self that we refuse to die to. "Do you think this passage means nothing? It says, 'The Spirit that lives in us wants us to be His own'" (James 4:5 NOG).

The sanctification of a believer is the process whereby the natural is overcome by the spiritual.

My brothers and sisters, I want you to be filled with the fullness of the Holy Spirit. He will help you to break out of your natural and will bring you into a new spiritual life you never could have imagined. Surrender to gain the victory. It will be the most glorious day in your life.

A Prayer for Surrendering to the Holy Spirit

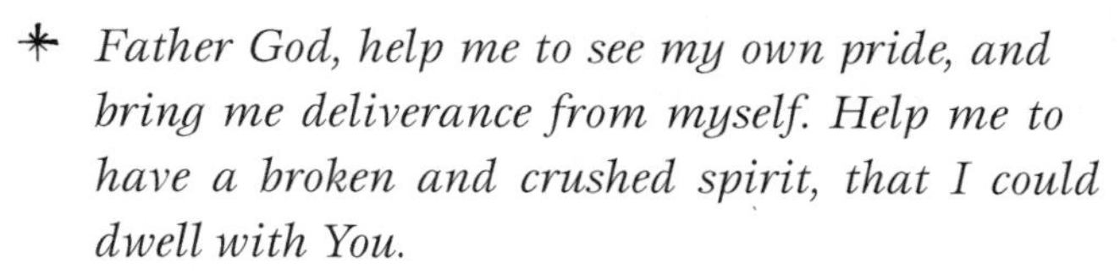

* *Father God, help me to see my own pride, and bring me deliverance from myself. Help me to have a broken and crushed spirit, that I could dwell with You.*

* *Lord Jesus, help me know how lowly and meek You are, that I could learn from You, be more like You, and come to You as a weak and broken soul in need of a Savior.*

* *Holy Spirit, I fall down and pray that You would fill me and teach me in all things. Teach me to be more like Jesus in every way, and help me to have His life reigning in me.*

Spiritual Guide

* If you don't already fast, then start. If you have medical issues, then fast from something besides food. When we fast, it denies our flesh so the Spirit can reign in us. Jesus did not teach "if you fast" but "when you fast." He said, "But when you fast, comb your hair and wash your face. Then no one will notice that you are fasting, except your Father, who knows what you do in private. And your Father, who sees everything, will reward you" (Matthew 6:17-18 NLT).

* Guard the gates of your mind to keep yourself pure for the Holy Spirit. Your eye gates and ear gates need to keep out whatever does not belong. Consider your conversations with people, as well as emails, internet browsing, TV, movies, music, books,

and anything else that gets into your mind, and pray that the Lord will show you whether it belongs there. It's easier to keep a thing out of your mind than it is to remove it once it gets in. "For I am the LORD your God. You shall therefore consecrate yourselves, and you shall be holy; for I am holy" (Leviticus 11:44).

* Learn to sacrifice your worries to the Lord. When we worry, we're carrying the load and not surrendering it to God. Surrendering our life is not a one-and-done thing, but a step-by-step process. So begin by surrendering those things you worry about. When we give Him our worries, it proves that we trust Him. Jesus taught, "So don't worry about these things, saying, 'What will we eat? What will we drink? What will we wear?' These things dominate the thoughts of unbelievers, but your heavenly Father already knows all your needs" (Matthew 6:31-32 NLT).

4

Changed by the Holy Spirit

Just as it takes the power of God to make man, it takes the power of God to change him.

"For God is working in you, giving you the desire and the power to do what pleases Him" (Philippians 2:13 NLT).

There's only so much you can do to change yourself. You cannot do what only God can do. It's your flesh that tells you to do the work. It's the devil who agrees with your flesh. The devil is a liar, and your flesh is no better. The Word does not say to transform yourself, but to "be transformed" (Romans 12:2).

If God thought you could do it on your own, why would He send His Son to die for your sins, and then send the Holy Spirit to give you power over your sins? God knows you better than you know yourself.

Stop telling God He can't change you—and just let Him.

Stop telling God He can't change you—and just let Him.

Regeneration is not a makeover but a do-over. The programs of man may fail, but the Holy Spirit never fails. "Not by works of righteousness which we have done, but according to His mercy He saved us, through the washing of regeneration and renewing of the Holy Spirit," (Titus 3:5).

To the degree that you control your life, the Lord does not.

To the degree that you control your life, the Lord does not.

Only the God who created all things can create a change in you. "Create in me a clean heart, O God, and renew a right and steadfast spirit within me" (Psalm 51:10 AMP).

I struggled for years to live for God. It was in the struggle that I was in error, since it was my pride trying to do the work that God alone could do in me. I know so many Christians who are still on this mouse-wheel of works, trying as hard as they can to live a life of victory. Child of God, the mouse-wheel of self-help will only wear you out and then leave you wanting.

The secret of living a life of victory is in surrendering your life to Him that His victory would be in you. Every time I fail, I know it's because I'm relying upon myself. Jesus never fails. When Jesus reigns in you, then He will be your victory. When you fail, turn to Him, confess it, and believe upon Him to help you. He promised us help with the Helper, the Holy Spirit.

Remove the idea that you can make yourself better. Let Him have His way with you. "Though outwardly we are wearing out, inwardly we are renewed day by day" (2 Corinthians 4:16 NOG).

People think that if they can become obedient, they will get filled with the Holy Spirit. It is the other way around. When you become filled by the Holy Spirit, then it is by His power alone that you can be obedient. The Lord promised us, "I will put my Spirit inside you and change you so that you will obey my laws. You will carefully obey my commands" (Ezekiel 36:27 ERV).

We need to stop praying that the Lord would change His mind, and pray instead that He will change ours.

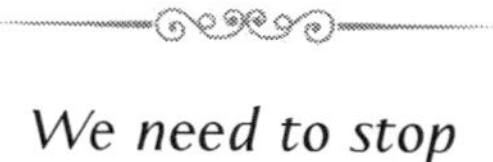

We need to stop praying that the Lord would change His mind, and pray instead that He will change ours.

We need to stop making excuses for why we cannot live a holy life, and just let Him live His holy life through us. "I have been crucified with Christ; it is no longer I who live, but Christ lives in me" (Galatians 2:20).

Join me in daring to live a life surrendered to Him—a life changed by the Holy Spirit. Be sure that God can change you. He has all the resources in heaven in which to make the changes. He has the knowledge of what needs to be changed. The only thing He needs is your permission. The Father is a gentleman, and He won't force His Spirit on you, but will wait until you're ready to receive Him.

To go from glory to glory, you will have to be changed. "As all of us reflect the Lord's glory with faces that are not covered with veils, we are being changed into His image with ever-increasing glory. This comes from the Lord, who is the Spirit" (2 Corinthians 3:18 NOG).

Glory is always upon glory. You must be on the first level of glory to reach the second.

Be obedient where you are now, and you will never remain there.

When I came to faith, I had all the zeal and energy to change myself. I sometimes even made great strides in several areas. I would think myself quite far along in my journey. But then, always, I would fail. Even if I didn't backslide, the Lord would show me how corrupt I was even at the level I'd attained.

The problem we have with our sin nature is that it's deeper than we ever imagined. It's so deep that only by the power of the Holy Spirit can we be changed. Until you truly understand the depth of your depravity—that only the Spirit of God can change you—you'll continue to either be a meager Christian or a Christian with a grand delusion about your own false view of self-holiness.

There are countless books written by man that will try to teach you how to change yourself. They take your money, give you empty words, and then leave you wanting more. Stop trying everything except God. Instead, see what God can do for you. If you want to be changed, the Holy Spirit is plan A, and there is no plan B.

If you want to be changed, the Holy Spirit is plan A, and there is no plan B.

Some of you need deliverance from your stack of books.

It is good to study the things of man, but without the Holy Spirit, you will never understand the things of God. "God has revealed them to us through His Spirit. For the Spirit searches all things, yes, the deep things of God" (1 Corinthians 2:10).

Hold God to His Word, and His Word will take hold of you. "He who calls you is faithful, who also will do it" (1 Thessalonians 5:24).

If you want to live a holy life, you must be willing to let the Holy Spirit live it through you. The only way you can be holy is to be dead to sin and alive to God. We have it all backward; we think we must try harder, but instead we must give up our life to Him. We can never gain what can only be given. So long as we try to take it, we aren't in a position to receive it.

Dead men don't sin. "So you also must consider yourselves dead to sin and alive to God in Christ Jesus" (Romans 6:11 ESV).

Never doubt that God can change you—but will you let Him?

To die to your natural self, you need the Holy Spirit to help you. "For if you live according to the flesh you will die; but if by the

Spirit you put to death the deeds of the body, you will live" (Romans 8:13).

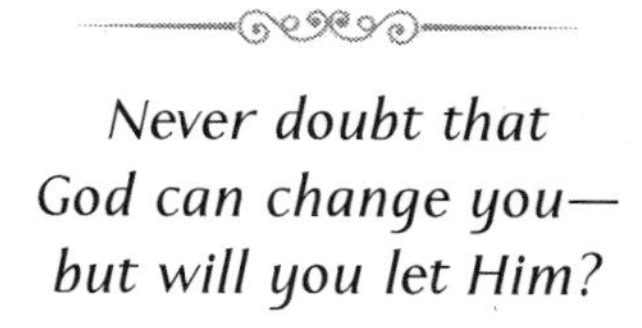

Never doubt that God can change you—but will you let Him?

Child of God, never doubt that the Father loves you. He sent His Son to die for you, and He sent the Holy Spirit to help you. It's up to you to receive the Son as your Savior; in the same way, it's up to you to receive the Holy Spirit as your Helper. Won't you pray for that today?

Don't be deceived by thinking you already have the fullness of the Holy Spirit. Certainly, if you're in Christ, the Holy Spirit is in you. But it's one thing to have the Holy Spirit in you, and something far different to have the fullness of the Holy Spirit reigning over every area of your life. Whenever you fail, either by your blatant sin or your prideful holiness, you have yet to surrender fully to the Spirit of God.

The Holy Spirit fills you to the degree that you let Him. "Do you not know that you are the temple of God and that the Spirit of God dwells in you?" (1 Corinthians 3:16).

You are meant to be the Father's son or daughter. "All who are led by God's Spirit are God's sons" (Romans 8:14 CJB).

The Holy Spirit fills you to the degree that you let Him.

My life has been so radically changed by the Holy Spirit that I barely recognize the man who looks back at me in the mirror each morning. Beloved child of God, you can be changed by the Holy Spirit. It doesn't matter how low you are, or how high you think you are—the Holy Spirit can still do a work in you. God's ability to change you is dependent not on your power but on your willingness. Be willing.

The Christian who receives more is the one who thirsts for more. The way you'll get more is to not settle for less. We have too many settled Christians. Fall to your knees and be willing to let the Spirit-filled life cost you something. Pray to be changed by the Holy Spirit. Pray for this, and don't be willing to stop until you get everything the Word of God has promised you.

A Prayer for Being Changed by the Holy Spirit

* *Father God, help me to see the change needed in me—not only the big things that can be noticed by men but also the small things that You see, those things hidden deep within my heart.*

* *Lord Jesus, teach me to live a lowly servant's life, humble in my spirit, gentle with my words, knowing where I came from, and forgiving others as You have forgiven me.*

* *Holy Spirit, I pray that I would be so willing to be changed by You that I experience an ongoing transformation from glory to glory, and to even more glory after that.*

Spiritual Guide

* Whatever sins you commit, bring them humbly before your Father and confess them one by one. There's no sin so small that it requires no confession. Don't try to hide anything, and once your sin is exposed, He will forgive you. "If we confess our sins, He is faithful and just to forgive us our sins and to cleanse us from all unrighteousness" (1 John 1:9).

* Stop the idea that you need to just try harder. That's the devil keeping you on the never-ending mouse-wheel of works, by which you'll never gain deliverance. Thank God for His gift of saving you. "For by grace you have been saved through faith, and that not of yourselves; it is the gift of God" (Ephesians 2:8).

* In however you fail, come before the Father and remind Him that He has promised to put His Spirit inside you and to help you live by His laws. Speak His Word out loud, and pray the promise over your life, so that both angels and demons will know the ground you're standing on. "I'll put my Spirit in you and make it possible for you to do what I tell you and live by My commands" (Ezekiel 36:27 MSG).

5

Convicted by the Holy Spirit

You have to be willing to be wrong that you can be made right.

Jesus said, "And when He [the Holy Spirit] has come, He will convict the world of sin" (John 16:8).

If you want to grow in the power of the Holy Spirit, then the Holy Spirit must have the right of way to convict you into holiness. We need holy lives into which He can pour His holy power. We live in a day when people want to have their ears tickled and their hearts entertained; what they really need is to have their ears boxed and their hearts pierced. If you want to go far in the Spirit-filled life, you must be prepared to be convicted by the Holy Spirit.

The value of a lesson learned is the lesson lived out.

The more you respond to the Holy Spirit, the more He will convict you.

So long as you are convicted by the Holy Spirit, you are on the right track. Jesus promised us, "When He, the Spirit of truth, has come, He will guide you into all truth" (John 16:13).

So long as you are convicted by the Holy Spirit, you are on the right track.

Several years ago, I was in a prison chapel, and just a few minutes away from preaching a message. I was having a conversation with another man in the prison ministry and was telling him about having recently gone into the hospital for a procedure. I mentioned that as they were about to put me under, the nurse asked if I had a "do not resuscitate" order in place, which I did not. I told my ministry friend what I was thinking just before being put under, "that if I ever went to heaven, they'd better not ever drag me back down to this miserable planet we live on. I love people here on earth, but I long to be in heaven with my Lord."

After I told him this story, he said something about it being a good word I'd spoken to this nurse. However, I hadn't said this out loud to her; I'd only thought it. I didn't correct him, and the service was just starting, so I let it go, thinking little of this short conversation.

I still remember what I preached that day; it was about walking with God. One of the things I mentioned was that our walk with God is evident in every choice we make; that every choice is either a step walking with God or a step away from God. I preached the same message in another yard on that prison later that day, and I went home late that afternoon. It was a very long but good day to serve the Lord.

That night I went to sleep, and soon I fell into a dream. In the dream, I walked into a beautiful white chapel. It looked so pure and holy. Inside the chapel, I saw a man and two women. I could tell that the man was a minister and that the women were also part of the church. To my shock, the three of them were doing lustful things that ought not be done, especially not in the house of God. I was very hurt by what I was watching. I couldn't believe what they were doing in the house of God, and I couldn't understand why this had come to me in a dream.

The dream ended, and I woke up in the middle of the night. I was lying there thinking how horrible the sight was that I'd just seen. I came from a dark past, and I don't recount this dream to elevate myself as being more holy or pure than another. But at this point in my walk with God, what I'd seen in my dream hurt me so much.

As I was wondering about what the dream meant, the Holy Spirit revealed the meaning to me. He showed me that what I did earlier that day—not correcting myself with that man about my story from the hospital—was a lie. Even a small lie is as dark as what I saw in my dream. I heard the sting of these words: *"How dare you sin in the house of God."* I felt the conviction from the Holy Spirit so harshly, so deeply, that it boxed my ears and pierced my heart.

Child of God, we have a Father in heaven who is merciful and who will forgive us of any sin. All we need do is confess it and repent from it and turn back to Him, and He'll swoop us up in His arms and make us clean as snow. But don't be deceived. He is a holy God, and He has sent His Holy Spirit to convict us into holiness. With however you believe grace allows you to remain in your sin, you're wrong. Let the Holy Spirit reveal where you're wrong, and He'll make you right in the eyes of the Father.

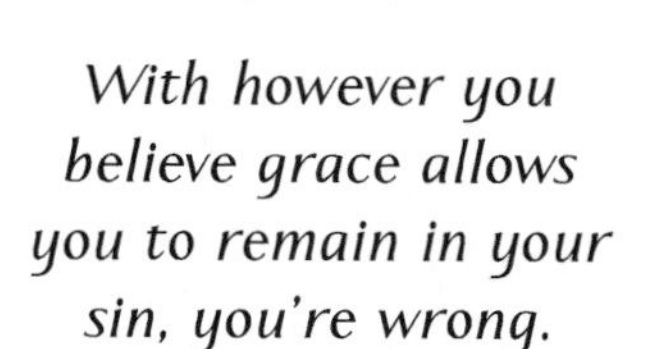
With however you believe grace allows you to remain in your sin, you're wrong.

We're covered in the righteousness of Christ and filled with the righteousness of the Holy Spirit. We need to be continuously changed by the conviction of the Holy Spirit, so that we can be the holy vessels set apart for God that we were meant to be.

The holier the man, the more convicted is his soul.

Be the one whom God can use to build His kingdom. "The Lord wants to use you for special purposes, so make yourself clean from all evil. Then you will be holy, and the Master can use you. You will be ready for any good work" (2 Timothy 2:21 ERV).

The holier the man, the more convicted is his soul.

The reason so few stand in victory is that so few kneel in humility.

The Word is not meant to condemn you about where you are, but to change you into who you were meant to be. It's not enough to feel convicted; you must also be changed.

What I've learned is that I should welcome the conviction of the Holy Spirit, because it means God is still doing a work in me. We all fall short of the glory of God, but God still reaches out to help us. Learn to let the sting of convictions take you closer to God and transform you into being more useful to the kingdom. The conviction isn't meant to shame us, but to shape us, to help mold us into the saints we were always meant to be. After the Lord rebuked me for my lie that I had done in the house of God, I've walked more carefully in what I tell others, making sure I explain myself completely.

The conviction isn't meant to shame us, but to shape us, to help mold us into the saints we were always meant to be.

Sometimes we need a harsh truth to reveal the smallest of sins. Learn to receive a harsh word, and allow it to do whatever surgery is needed within you. The kingdom is depending upon you to live a holy life so that your life will be more useful to God in reaching friends, family, and others around you. If you want to walk in the power of the

Holy Spirit, first be prepared to be convicted by the Holy Spirit so that any power He puts upon you will be received in humility and fear. The power from the Holy Spirit is reserved for those broken enough to be used by the Holy Spirit.

I was praying to the Lord about wanting to understand more about what it means to be convicted by the Holy Spirit. This doesn't happen all the time, but I started to receive a very long word about what I was praying for. I started to record onto my iPhone app, and below is only the beginning of all that I received. Child of God, believe that the Lord is with us and that the Holy Spirit can give us a word. Stay in prayer so that your life has ears by which you can hear Him and have a heart to understand Him.

Here's what I received, except that I've added some verses to go with it:

If you want the Holy Spirit to fall upon you, then you must kneel down into a position by which you can receive Him.

Nobody filled with the Holy Spirit is excused from being convicted by the Holy Spirit. "Behold, happy is the man whom God corrects; therefore do not despise the chastening of the Almighty" (Job 5:17).

Jesus said the Holy Spirit will come and convict the world of sin. You're in the world, and you need to be convicted of your sin. If you want to walk in the power of the Holy Spirit and in the gifts of the Holy Spirit, then you especially need to be convicted into holiness. "And when He [the Holy Spirit] has come, He will convict the world of sin" (John 16:8).

Nobody filled with the Holy Spirit is excused from being convicted by the Holy Spirit

Never think you're so far along that you don't need a rebuke. The ones who go astray from God are the ones who stop listening to His rebukes. You need to be convicted so that you can be made into something new. "Put on the new man which was created according to God, in true righteousness and holiness" (Ephesians 4:24).

You need to be convicted so that you can be made into something new.

Sometimes the conviction of the Holy Spirit is not to correct us in where we're wrong, but to prevent us from going where we aren't supposed to go.

Sometimes the conviction is because we have not gone where we should have gone. The sins of omission are sometimes greater than the sins of commission, because they cause us not to do all that God would have us do. "Therefore, to him who knows to do good and does not do it, to him it is sin" (James 4:17).

When the Holy Spirit tells you not to go somewhere, don't go there. "They were forbidden by the Holy Spirit to preach the word in Asia" (Acts 16:6).

When the Holy Spirit tells you to go somewhere, go there. "Then the Spirit said to Philip, 'Go near and overtake this chariot'" (Acts 8:29).

If the Holy Spirit wants to transport you, let Him transport you. "Now when they came up out of the water, the Spirit of the Lord caught Philip away, so that the eunuch saw him no more" (Acts 8:39).

If the Holy Spirit is going to give you a word to say, let Him do so. "Paul was compelled by the Spirit, and testified to the Jews that Jesus is the Christ" (Acts 18:5).

If the Holy Spirit comes upon you and tells you to rip a lion apart with your bare hands, just step into it and do it. "And the Spirit of the LORD came mightily upon him, and he tore the lion apart as one would have torn apart a young goat, though he had nothing in his hand" (Judges 14:6).

Stop questioning the Lord and His abilities, and start trusting in Him and in all that He can do in you.

Stop questioning the Lord and His abilities, and start trusting in Him and in all that He can do in you.

This message I received kept going on for quite some time. Perhaps someday I can share the rest of it. What I have learned in my spiritual journey is that the Lord must first prepare the vessel, and then the vessel is ready for Him to pour into it. Godly conviction is always restorative in purpose and loving in nature. Stay diligent in your spiritual growth to let the Lord prepare you.

A Prayer for the Holy Spirit's Conviction

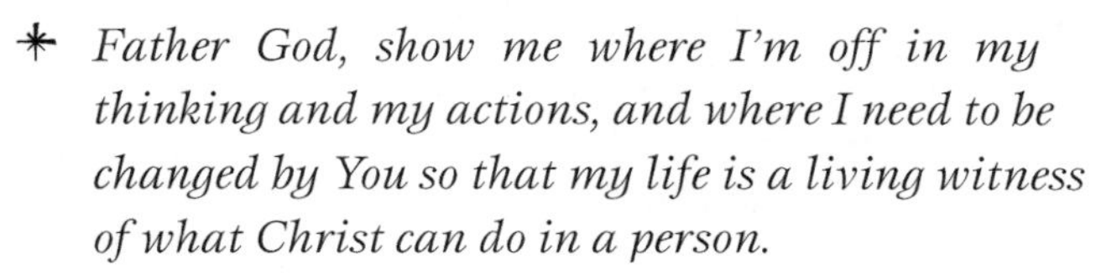

* *Father God, show me where I'm off in my thinking and my actions, and where I need to be changed by You so that my life is a living witness of what Christ can do in a person.*

* *Lord Jesus, show me where I'm still selfish and prideful, more worried about what man thinks of me than about what You know about me. Help me to be meek but mighty.*

* *Holy Spirit, I ask You to convict me into the heart and will of the Father and the Son, making me a useful utensil for building the kingdom of God, to the glory of Jesus Christ.*

Spiritual Guide

* Never think yourself above or below anyone else—young or old, timid or bold, rich or poor. Think of yourself as just another soul who falls short of the glory of God. "Therefore,

if you have any encouragement for me from your being in union with the Messiah, any comfort flowing from love, any fellowship with me in the Spirit, or any compassion and sympathy, then complete my joy by having a common purpose and a common love, by being one in heart and mind" (Philippians 2:1-2 CJB).

* Pray that the realization of the promises of Jesus would come upon you. The power is not only through you but to change you so that you can be an instrument of God. Jesus said, "But you shall receive power when the Holy Spirit has come upon you" (Acts 1:8).

* In however you serve at your church, even if by prayer in the back row, determine that you will be a vessel of God, filled by the Holy Spirit, and effective in ministering to those around you. "Don't get drunk with wine, because it makes you lose control. Instead, keep on being filled with the Spirit" (Ephesians 5:18 CJB).

6 You Shall Receive Power

Holy Spirit power does not come by taking but by receiving.

Jesus taught us, "You shall receive power when the Holy Spirit has come upon you" (Acts 1:8).

I've always had a sense of inadequacy in doing ministry. When I minister alongside others, I'm always glad to just sit to the side and be nothing. When I'm called to minister on my own, whether by speaking or with writing, I'm helpless to do anything of my own power. How much we need more servants in ministry who stop trying to minister on their own power.

I used to think I could never do anything of value on my own for God. Now I'm far more certain of that. I've learned more about the Word of God, and on some days I can even be a little clever. But what I've come to learn is that the best thing we can be is helpless before the Lord. We'll seek the Lord in our weakness but not in our strength. Learn to be weak so that God is your strength.

This inadequacy in myself has forced me to plead with the Lord that He would help me. In however I serve Him, I fall helplessly before Him and pray for the power of the Holy Spirit to help me. I've agonized for hours before the Lord, pleading for Him to help me. He has never failed me. The secret of the power of the Holy Spirit is that it comes only by receiving and not by our attaining.

The secret of the power of the Holy Spirit is that it comes only by receiving and not by our attaining.

Jesus did not say take hold of the power, rather He said, "You shall receive power" (Acts 1:8).

Some people teach that the indwelling of the Holy Spirit is a one-and-done experience that happens at conversion, and there's nothing more after that. I'm so sad when people teach that, since I believe they're teaching only to the level of their own meager experience with the Holy Spirit.

There's an indwelling of the Holy Spirit at our conversion, for it's the Spirit who does the work in the heart of a new believer. But there's a greater filling and an ongoing filling available to those who dare to receive it. We must ask that we might receive. Pray each day for a greater filling of the Holy Spirit, and watch what God will do with that.

Listen to the Word of God more than to those who water it down to match their own meager spiritual experience. Many well-meaning teachers try to limit the Holy Spirit to the detriment of those they're teaching. Whenever in doubt, the Word of God trumps all. Start believing the Word of God more than the word of man. You need the Spirit of God to teach you the Word of God. Ask the Holy Spirit to teach you.

Whenever in doubt, the Word of God trumps all.

Scripture shows us that the Holy Spirit upon us is not a one-and-done experience. It wasn't that way for the disciples, and if it wasn't that way for them, you can be sure the same is true for you and me.

Before Jesus ascended, He did this for the disciples: "He breathed on them, and said to them, 'Receive the Holy Spirit'" (John 20:22).

Sometime later, Jesus also told the disciples, "You shall be baptized with the Holy Spirit not many days from now" (Acts 1:5).

And then Jesus said, "You shall receive power when the Holy Spirit has come upon you" (Acts 1:8).

After Jesus ascended, something wonderful happened on Pentecost day: "And they were all filled with the Holy Spirit" (Acts 2:4).

Many days later some of the disciples were praying, and yet again something wonderful happened: "And when they had prayed, the place where they were assembled together was shaken; and they were all filled with the Holy Spirit, and they spoke the word of God with boldness" (Acts 4:31).

The disciples received the Holy Spirit three times in these verses—and also, I would propose, a hundred more times than this. How much we need to keep pressing into the fullness of the Holy Spirit within us!

Many people are so convinced that they've received the fullness of the Holy Spirit that they don't seek anything more, and so they get nothing more. Jesus taught, "How much more will your heavenly Father give the Holy Spirit to those who ask and continue to ask Him!" (Luke 11:13 AMP).

We get into doctrinal arguments over things that are so simple. We need to read the Word and have it revealed to us by the Holy

Spirit, so that there is greater unity in the church. Our problem is that we trust the commentaries of man more than commentary from the Holy Spirit.

If you want a movement of the Holy Spirit around you, you must first have a movement of the Holy Spirit within you.

On occasion, someone who's quite smart and a naturally gifted speaker will try to give me a lesson on the things of God. They'll go on at great length with whatever doctrine or opinion they're trying to teach me. But I'll see in them the arrogance of man and an emptiness of the Spirit of God. Even if their general argument is correct, there's no power in it. It's as if they're trying to show me light from a candle, but they fail to simply light the candle that we might both see it. I pray for such people that they would learn not to be adequate in themselves, that they would simply fall down before a God who is so much higher, and that He would put the fullness of His Spirit within them.

The more you empty yourself, the more the Holy Spirit can fill you. "And they were all filled with the Holy Spirit" (Acts 2:4).

Your thirst for the Holy Spirit determines how much you will drink. The Lord Jesus said, "If anyone thirsts, let him come to Me and drink....this He spoke concerning the Spirit, whom those believing in Him would receive" (John 7:37,39).

Your thirst for the Holy Spirit determines how much you will drink.

I can tell when a message is given only by the power of man. It sounds good, but moves little. It is sometimes clever, but always shallow. It has gimmicks but no gumption. It stirs the flesh but not the spirit. It impresses man, but does not change him. It will draw more laughs than tears.

It makes more friends than saints. It makes people feel comfortable as they are. It takes more effort to prepare than to deliver, but delivers less and prepares nothing. It pleases men more than teaches them. It tastes good but nourishes little. It sounds nice but has no power.

It tries to take earth to heaven instead of bringing heaven down to earth. It is born of flesh and has no life of the Spirit. It does not upset the elders or the unsaved, which in some cases are one and the same. It was born out of the tombs of men's offices and not wrestled for in the prayer closet alone with God.

Oh, what I would give to see more weak and feeble preachers on earth who have no choice but to rely upon our God! You can give a word of the Lord only if the Lord Himself has given a word to you. I learned a long time ago that I cannot do anything of kingdom value without the Holy Spirit's power upon me. The same is true for you.

The problem we have is never God's limit in giving; rather, it's our limit in receiving. "Now we have received, not the spirit of the world, but the Spirit who is from God, that we might know the things that have been freely given to us by God" (1 Corinthians 2:12).

The problem we have is never God's limit in giving; rather, it's our limit in receiving.

When I taught or preached in prisons, before going in I would fast and pray, then right before going in I would fall down before God and plead with Him to pour out His Spirit upon me. And pour out He did. I don't say this to promote myself, but to promote the Holy Spirit and what He can do for you. He has never failed me, and friend, He will never fail you.

Don't think you need this greater filling of the Holy Spirit only if you're preaching to many. We can barely remember the message we heard at a service a week ago, but when a servant of God gives us a word one on one, we carry it for a lifetime. You're meant to be that servant to somebody. We need the Holy Spirit to minister to even one. Your ministry is wherever you are. And wherever you are, you need the Holy Spirit to do a mighty work through you.

Over the years, I've been extremely blessed to experience many divine appointments. I never know when these will happen, and

God places someone before me that He might minister to them through me, or minister to me through them. Sometimes He uses us and we don't even know. We don't need to always know, but we need to always be willing.

There are souls on this planet you are destined to minister to. Faith stirs up faith. We need to be willing to submit to those around us that we might be stirred by them. We also must be willing to stir up the faith in those around us.

When you're tapping into the resources of heaven, there will be nothing on earth that can stop you. "My help comes from the LORD, who made heaven and earth" (Psalm 121:2).

When you're tapping into the resources of heaven, there will be nothing on earth that can stop you.

It's a wonderful thing to realize you don't have to serve Him in your own power. If you want to start a movement, let Him move in you, then *be* the movement. Make it your mission to be the one in your circle of influence who inspires others to be filled with the fullness of the Holy Spirit. Yield yourself to the Spirit so you can be a utensil for God.

It's not enough to only receive power; it must flow through us onto others. It doesn't need to be spectacular before men, but useful for the plans of God. Believe that God can still do miracles, and that He chooses to do them in His grace through ordinary people like you and me. Sometimes the greatest miracle is that He would even use us.

Be sure that when He uses you, it's not because of who you are, but who He is. Remain humble in whatever He would do through you. Your humility will allow the river to keep flowing through you. *A river flows only when the ground has given way.*

A Prayer for Receiving Power

* *Father God, help me to be so weak in myself that I can then be filled with Your strength. Show me to be so dependent upon You that I never rely upon myself for anything You would have me do.*

* *Lord Jesus, show me wherever I seek power for my own glory and help me turn away from it. I would rather be weak and humble before You than strong and proud before men.*

* *Holy Spirit, help me to be humble enough to be used by the Father to the glory of the Son. Help me realize I'm only a utensil in the hands of God. Help me to be useful to the kingdom.*

Spiritual Guide

* You must learn to think yourself nothing so that He can do something through you. God said, "The kind of person on whom I look with favor is one with a poor and humble spirit, who trembles at My word" (Isaiah 66:2).

* Pray that God will give you only the power that would not cause you to become prideful. When we serve God, our greatest danger is that we might want to claim some of His glory. "For many walk, of whom I have told you often, and now tell you even weeping, that they are the enemies of the cross of Christ: whose end is destruction, whose god is their belly, and whose glory is in their shame—who set their mind on earthly things" (Philippians 3:18-19).

* Never exaggerate what the Lord has said or done in your life, because that is your pride, and it has no place in the kingdom of God. A half-truth is a lie, and lies are rotten fruit. "(for the fruit of the Spirit is in all goodness, righteousness, and truth)" (Ephesians 5:9).

7

Baptism of the Holy Spirit

When you are filled by the Holy Spirit, you are no longer just a man or a woman.

John the Baptist told the people, "I indeed baptize you with water; but One mightier than I is coming, whose sandal strap I am not worthy to loose. He will baptize you with the Holy Spirit and fire" (Luke 3:16).

We learn in Scripture about the baptism of the Holy Spirit and how Jesus would be the One to give it to us. Many think that this is a one-and-done experience, and there's nothing more. I can assure you there is something more.

Child of God, our faith journey is a daily process of denying our flesh and being filled with the Holy Spirit. But there's that first great filling of the Holy Spirit called the baptism of the Holy Spirit, in which the power and fullness of the Holy Spirit first comes upon us.

For some, this baptism may come at conversion. From my experience, and that of most others I know, it comes later. I've heard many argue about the timing, and I caution you not to question God on when He might do a work in you. I pray that everyone would gain this most wonderful blessed gift from the Father.

Below is my story. I pray it would encourage you to share your own experience with others, or to press in and someday have an experience of your own.

I want you to know that there's something great and wonderful in the baptism of the Holy Spirit. Nothing can compare to this moment in the life of a believer. It's the day that God moves in. It's the day that heaven fills you. It's the day that the Spirit moves you. It's a day you'll never forget.

There's something great and wonderful in the baptism of the Holy Spirit.

Being baptized in the Holy Spirit is not the finish line of your faith, but the catapult from which it will flourish.

This is not a matter of salvation, since we can be saved but not yet baptized in the Holy Spirit. "For as yet He [the Holy Spirit] had fallen upon none of them. They had only been baptized in the name of the Lord Jesus. Then they laid hands on them, and they received the Holy Spirit" (Acts 8:16-17).

If you've been baptized in the Spirit, that's a great blessing you've received. If you desire this baptism, I want to encourage you to keep seeking it. And if you don't believe in it, then I pray you would read through the Scriptures, praying for the Holy Spirit to bring you a revelation of this truth.

There's more to God than you know. Never limit your mind by the minds of other men, but seek the mind of Christ. "For 'who has known the mind of the Lord that he may instruct Him?' But we have the mind of Christ" (1 Corinthians 2:16).

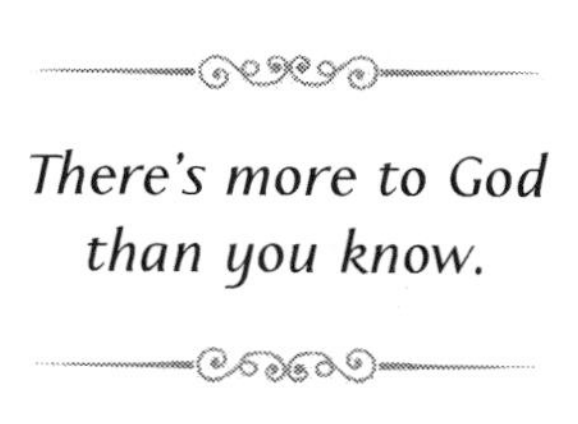
There's more to God than you know.

For some years, I was teaching and preaching in prison ministry. I was blessed to meet some mighty servants filled with the power of the Holy Spirit, and to be mentored by them. Yet I had little of this power of the Holy Spirit within me. I could argue doctrines better than I could live them. I could preach on power, but I couldn't step down from the podium and walk in this power.

I was striving to gain something more. I longed to live a life higher than I was able to live. I wanted to have what I saw others had. I wanted to live as high as I preached. I longed to have a deeper, more intimate relationship with the Lord. I wanted to be useful in the hands of God.

Then there was a day I'll never forget. May we all be blessed to have such a day! I'd been doing ministry for several days in a row, going into a few different prisons to serve. I'd been teaching and preaching—on what, I don't remember. In those days, my teaching was based mostly on human power and had little Holy Spirit power behind it.

I'd been fasting from food and was on my third day of not eating. Child of God, I want you to know that if you're going to get closer to God, you must move further away from yourself. If you aren't willing to sacrifice, then what is it you have to give? We must learn to rule over our natural by His supernatural within us. The secret power found through praying combined with fasting is something everyone would be most blessed to discover.

I went to a Spirit-filled meeting, and it was extraordinary. I could feel the presence of the Holy Spirit in this place. I could see the Holy Spirit moving in the man leading this meeting. I'll never forget the encounter I had with this man of God.

I stayed in the back for the first few hours of this meeting. I'm content to always stay in the back, since I'm not comfortable being noticed or being around people. Later in the meeting, I was ministering in the back row to a young man with autism. I was just praying for him. We think we must do more than prayer, but with faith, prayer is enough. I asked this young man if he wanted to go up to the front so that the ministry team could pray for him too. He agreed and so I took him up there.

While I was up at the front, the man of God motioned for me to come over to him. When he was near me, he just breathed out on me, and I instantly collapsed and could not get back up. It was as if the Holy Spirit poured out over me, and I was overwhelmed by His presence upon me. Child of God, when the Spirit of the Lord comes upon you, the weight of glory is greater than you can bear.

When the Spirit of the Lord comes upon you, the weight of glory is greater than you can bear.

I was finally able to start getting back up, and as I was trying to do so, this man of God turned back to me and waved his hand, and I felt the Spirit of God overwhelm me again. I collapsed backward to the ground. It was the most wonderful, warming, comforting, and peaceful experience I've ever had. It was as if a heavenly wave washed over me, cleansed me, filled me, and then forever changed me.

I cannot explain the theology of that moment, but I felt it as sure as I feel the warmth from the sun. I was overwhelmed by the baptism of the Holy Spirit upon me, like a wave of the goodness of God. I can explain this experience no better than I can explain an infinite God.

This moment divides my whole life into before this experience and all that has happened after. I have truly lived and experienced the verse, "I will put My Spirit within you" (Ezekiel 36:27).

Child of God, we need to stop putting God in a box in how He might move in the life of a believer. I can tell you that from that day forward, the Holy Spirit began to manifest in my life in a hundred ways, too many to mention here in this one book. In preaching or writing, I'll occasionally tell of some of my experiences. But I don't want to just tell people how great it is, and to be some interesting showpiece. No, I want to help others get there. There are no limits with the resources of heaven. There's room in the Holy Spirit for all.

We need to stop putting God in a box in how He might move in the life of a believer.

The trajectory of my life was changed that day. I was moved from living in the wisdom of man to walking in the revelations found only in the wisdom of God. I could see what I couldn't see before. I could hear what I couldn't hear before. We think we must do a great thing to grow in our faith, but we're wrong. He must do a great work in us for us to grow in our faith.

Child of God, if you don't know whether you have the fullness of the Holy Spirit, then go after it until you do know. Jesus said there would be power. If there's no power, then keep pressing in until there is.

If you don't walk by the power of the Holy Spirit, then you are on your own. "And by this we know that He abides in us, by the Spirit whom He has given us" (1 John 3:24).

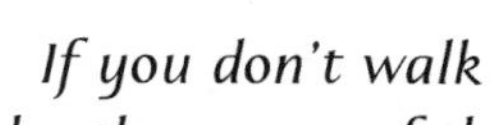

If you don't walk by the power of the Holy Spirit, then you are on your own.

There's no qualification to being filled by the Holy Spirit other than being saved, being willing, and then you're poured into. This pouring into you is not by the person pouring; rather it is only through them. The Lord said, "I will put My Spirit within you" (Ezekiel 36:27). God puts His Spirit in you.

Don't you want it? Don't you long for it? Can't you sense something is missing? You must know that it's God's will that you would have it. "So don't be foolish with your lives, but learn what the Lord wants you to do. Don't be drunk with wine, which will ruin your life, but be filled with the Spirit" (Ephesians 5:17-18 ERV).

If you're filled with the Holy Spirit, stop limiting yourself to only your abilities. Don't lower the bar to your own abilities, but raise the bar to His. Between me and the Holy Spirit, He can do anything!

Don't lower the bar to your own abilities, but raise the bar to His.

If you are a minister who is already filled, and you want to lay hands or breath out that someone may be filled, never think you can cause anything. Stop the processes and just be the utensil in His hands. You need to get out of the way. It's the Holy Spirit through you who moves onto the one you're laying hands on. And if you want to do it for your glory, then stop, before He stops you.

Oh, my friends, I pray that you would have this great baptism of the Holy Spirit!

A Prayer for the Baptism of the Holy Spirit

* *Father God, help me to see Your plan to fill me with the fullness of Your Spirit—that as I grow in my faith from glory to glory, I need only to keep pressing in for all that You would give me.*

* *Lord Jesus, I need the power and fullness of the Holy Spirit. It was promised that You would baptize us with the Holy Spirit; help me to be willing to be filled more and more each day.*

* *Holy Spirit, I want more. Each day I want to pray for a greater filling of You in my life, that I would deny my flesh daily, and be filled with You—so that by Your power my life can be changed forever.*

Spiritual Guide

* Each morning, pray that the Lord will help you to deny your flesh. If you want to have a greater filling of the Holy Spirit, you must yield more of your life to Him. "Those who are dominated by the sinful nature think about sinful things, but those who are controlled by the Holy Spirit think about things that please the Spirit" (Romans 8:5 NLT).

* Each morning, pray that the Father will give you a filling of the Holy Spirit. Before you do anything in the day, pray that the Holy Spirit will fill you and help you. Jesus taught, "If imperfect parents know how to lovingly take care of their children and give them what they need, how much more will the perfect heavenly Father give the Holy Spirit's fullness when his children ask him" (Luke 11:13 TPT).

* Find others who have the Spirit-filled life or are seeking it, and pray with them, believing upon the power of God manifested in the Holy Spirit here on earth. "And when they had prayed, the place where they were meeting together was shaken [a sign of God's presence]; and they were all filled with the Holy Spirit and began to speak the word of God with boldness and courage" (Acts 4:31 AMP).

8

Baptism of Fire

Where there is fire, there is light.

John the Baptist said of Jesus, "He will baptize you with the Holy Spirit and fire" (Matthew 3:11).

We often think of fire as destructive, but God uses fire for the kingdom. Fire is different things to different people. The light from fire is a joy to a believer but is terrible to those wanting to live in their darkness. Fire removes impurities—to the joy of a believer but to the dismay of an unbeliever.

When Israel was rescued out of Egypt, "The Lord went before them by day in a pillar of cloud to lead the way, and by night in a pillar of fire to give them light" (Exodus 13:21). This same pillar of fire was judgment for the Egyptians: "The Lord looked down upon the army of the Egyptians through the pillar of fire and cloud, and He troubled the army of the Egyptians" (Exodus 14:24).

Fire is judgment because light exposes the dark. "For everyone practicing evil hates the light and does not come to the light, lest his deeds should be exposed" (John 3:20).

Fire is judgment because light exposes the dark.

I was once in a season of an intense pressing in for the deeper things of God. I'd been pressing in more because I wanted more. I was in prayer asking for a word. I pray to receive more understanding, and when He answers those prayers, the floodgates sometimes open. Right away, I started to record on my iPhone app, and below is an excerpt of the Holy Spirit download I received. I've added verses, since I always want to qualify what I hear from the Spirit of God with what's in the Word of God. I don't question the Spirit of God; I question only whether I'm hearing Him clearly.

Here's a portion of what I recorded that day:

Fire is consuming. "For our God is a consuming fire" (Hebrews 12:29).

Fire is changing.

Fire is moving.

Fire is light.

Fire is purifying.

Step into it. You can have a greater faith. You can have a higher faith.

Don't listen to the enemy. He will tell you that you can't do it. He will remind you of who you were. He will tell you that you will never get there.

The Lord Jesus would have never commanded it if you couldn't do it. Jesus commanded us, "Therefore you shall be perfect, just as your Father in heaven is perfect" (Matthew 5:48).

Jesus made this bold statement: "If you love Me, keep My commandments" (John 14:15).

You can't do it on your own, but the Holy Spirit can do it in you. But you have to let Him do it in you, or else it won't happen.

You can't do it on your own, but the Holy Spirit can do it in you.

Jesus went on to tell us we are not on our own with this: "And I will pray the Father, and He will give you another Helper [the Holy Spirit], that He may abide with you forever" (John 14:16).

You can talk about it, and you can go through the programs of man all you want, but you can't change you. The Lord promised us, "I will put my Spirit inside you and cause you to live by my laws, respect my rulings and obey them" (Ezekiel 36:27 CJB).

You can't do surgery on your inside, because you would die trying. It won't work; you will never get there.

Just lay yourself up on that altar and say, "Lord, You do that work in me." Say, "I surrender to you Holy Spirit," and you mean it, and you just keep doing it. "Present your bodies a living sacrifice, holy, acceptable to God, which is your reasonable service" (Romans 12:1).

And if you fall, you just get back up. You fall down seven times; you get back up seven times. "For a righteous man may fall seven times and rise again…" (Proverbs 24:16).

And you keep dropping yourself on that potter's wheel, asking God to do the work on you. Plead with Him. Pray for it. Press into it. Be fervent. Go after it. You can have it. "And the vessel that he made of clay was marred in the hand of the potter; so he made it again into another vessel, as it seemed good to the potter to make" (Jeremiah 18:4).

People have gotten to the higher faith not because they are special, but because God is special, and they realize that.

If you look at the Beatitudes in Matthew 5:3-10, you will find they are the ladder of faith. The very first step in the ladder is: "Blessed are the poor in spirit, for theirs is the kingdom of heaven" (Matthew 5:3).

The very first thing that must happen to grow in your faith is that you must be poor in spirit. That means you are impoverished. You are nothing. You have nothing.

All you can do is fall down at the foot of the cross and plead for the blood of Jesus to cover you—that you might be something, and the only something that you will ever be is Christ in you. "To them God willed to make known what are the riches of the glory of this mystery among the Gentiles: which is Christ in you" (Colossians 1:27).

You must humiliate yourself into realizing that only in Christ, and in Christ alone, are you anything. He is your everything. Fall down before Him and let Him do the work in you.

You need to stop looking for organized religion to organize God into you.

You need to get over yourself. You need to stop looking for organized religion to organize God into you. What you need is between you and God. "That He would grant you, according to the riches of His glory, to be strengthened with might through His Spirit in the inner man" (Ephesians 3:16).

Stop thinking you're going to wake up someday and suddenly be strong enough. You're never going to be strong enough. You weren't strong enough yesterday or the day before or the week before. What makes you think anything's going to change? "But God has chosen the foolish things of the world to put to shame the wise, and God has chosen the weak things of the world to put to shame the things which are mighty" (1 Corinthians 1:27).

The definition of insanity is doing the same thing over and over and expecting you're going to get a different result. How many programs are you going to go to until you figure out the only way God will do a great work in you is when you let Him.

Stop thinking you must be smart to be strong. Jesus didn't go out and find the smartest guys to be filled with the Holy Spirit. He went out and found the willing guys. He knew they would be willing to be filled with the Holy Spirit because they knew they didn't have it in them to be what He was calling them up to be. And you don't have it either. "Not by might nor by power, but by My Spirit, says the LORD of hosts [angelic armies]" (Zechariah 4:6).

What will it take to get this into that thick skull of yours? You need to just fall down before Him. You need to pray like the disciples for ten days until you have your Pentecostal experience, and the Holy Spirit comes upon you. "These all continued with one accord in prayer.... And suddenly there came a sound from heaven... And they were all filled with the Holy Spirit" (Acts 1:14, 2:2,4).

There's a whole lot of people who have their starched shirts and polished shoes, but they don't have a lick of the Holy Spirit in them. All they have is the polished utensils of men on the outside. What we need is the flaming fire of the Holy Spirit on the inside. "He will baptize you with the Holy Spirit and fire" (Luke 3:16).

People think we can organize for what could happen and collect enough money to make it happen. The disciples just went into that room and prayed for ten days until the Holy Spirit came upon them, and then just let Him tear things up.

The problem we have today is people won't even gather to pray for ten minutes, let alone ten days.

We need saints who are willing to just go into a room and pray that the Holy Spirit will come upon them, that something would actually change. What are you waiting for?

Every fire starts with a spark. Let just one little spark ignite the fire in your life. Then the Holy Spirit will come alive in you.

The problem we have today is people won't even gather to pray for ten minutes, let alone ten days.

Why not you? Why not today? Why not right now?

Devote yourself. Dedicate yourself. Be determined in your will, your heart, and your mind—then watch what the Holy Spirit will do with that!

That was the end of the download. My prayer is to see people live a life filled with the power of the Holy Spirit pouring into them and then pouring out through them. If you already have this in your life, help others get it into theirs. If you don't yet have this in your life, keep persevering until you do. The promise of the Holy Spirit is for us all.

The promise of the Holy Spirit is for us all.

So many wonderful blessings can come from the Holy Spirit being active in your life. Not just blessings for you, but through you. Gaining the Holy Spirit is not meant to promote you, but to promote God through you onto others. When you're properly being used by the Holy Spirit, it won't even matter to you if you realize all the ways in which you're being used. We must seek to be selfless and minister in obscurity; from there we can bring all glory to God and be effective for the kingdom.

Yet there will be times when the Lord will bless you with revelation knowledge of how He has used you. Just before the Lord called me out of prison ministry, I was speaking with an inmate on one prison yard who gave me a gift from God. He was reminding me of a night when I'd come to open the prison chapel so the men could watch a movie. I'd been fasting from all media for many years, and so I sat in the chaplain's office as they watched their movie. I was quite tired that night, totally exhausted from not sleeping the night before. I was content just to be alone and in the Word.

Then the chaplain's clerk called me out to speak for a bit and to close in prayer. I asked how long I had to speak, figuring there were just a few minutes left. He said I had forty minutes. Isn't God the grandest orchestrator to take us out of ourselves so that He can then do a work through us? I find He often allows me to be exhausted before He will work through me, since it gets me out of His way.

I remember the clerk showing me a man who was suffering from some illness. I don't remember what the illness was, only that it was something with his lungs. I asked him to come up, and I laid hands on him and prayed for him to be healed. Why do we make it harder than that? Then he sat down.

I spoke for a little bit, and then I told the men that often God would show me who would be saved, but on this night I was just too tired. I told the men, "So if you're ready to be saved, then you just need to raise your hand." Immediately a hand went up. It was that man who I'd prayed over earlier to be healed. He came up, and that night he received the Lord Jesus Christ into his heart. That's the grandest healing a man can receive.

I never saw him again after that night. The inmate who was reminding me of this story told me about what happened to this man after that night. He became a burning flame in the church on that prison yard. Later he was transferred to another prison, and he became a flame in the church located there. At the new prison, he became the pastor on the yard, evangelizing and ministering to the other inmates every day. He led many men to salvation.

Sometimes the Lord allows us to see how He has used us so we'll be encouraged in everything else He would have us do. I didn't do anything to help that man, because I was too tired. But God can use us if we show up. You don't always get to see the fruit, but keep planting seeds anyway.

You don't always get to see the fruit, but keep planting seeds anyway.

Child of God, if you want to serve the Lord to the fullest, then you need to be filled with the Holy Spirit to the fullest, that He would have the right of way to minister through you. Your ministry is not *your* ministry but His ministry through you. Once you get that, then you'll be a blessing to the kingdom.

A Prayer for Being Baptized in Fire

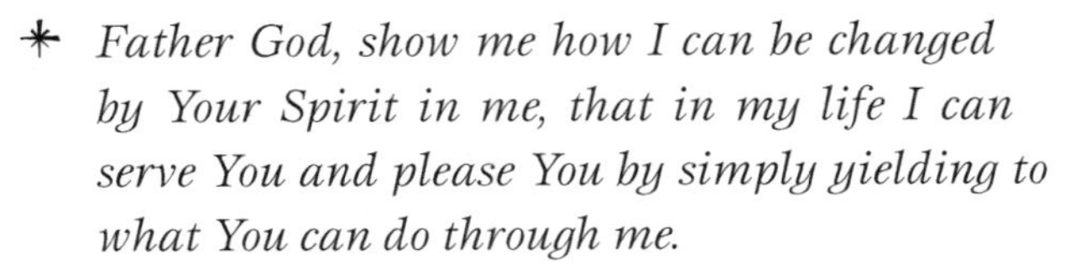

* *Father God, show me how I can be changed by Your Spirit in me, that in my life I can serve You and please You by simply yielding to what You can do through me.*

* *Lord Jesus, help me to see that it's by You alone that I can be baptized with the Holy Spirit and with fire—that this fire can purify me and prepare me to serve You with all my heart.*

* *Holy Spirit, I pray for Your fire to burn brightly in me, that by Your power my life will be changed, and that I can be a utensil in the Father's hands by Your power through me to the glory of Christ Jesus.*

Spiritual Guide

* Don't allow the traditions of man to have more weight than the truth of God. Spend more time in God's Word so that His Word will have more influence in you and then through you. "These [the Bereans] were more fair-minded than those in Thessalonica, in that they received the word with all readiness, and searched the Scriptures daily to find out whether these things were so" (Acts 17:11).

* Spend more time in the presence of God. Nobody can give you what comes from the Lord alone. "Now it came to pass in those days that He [Jesus] went out to the mountain to pray, and continued all night in prayer to God" (Luke 6:12). If Jesus needed to pray all night, how much more do we need to pray?

* Understand that God isn't limited by your understanding or your imagination. He will move in a variety of ways, and you just need to keep your mind open to what God is doing around you every day. "He reveals deep and secret things; He knows what is in the darkness, and light dwells with Him" (Daniel 2:22).

9

Led by the Holy Spirit

Stop acting like an orphan when you're called to be a son.

"All who are led by God's Spirit are God's sons" (Romans 8:14 CJB).

I had the great privilege to serve in prison ministry for fourteen years. In the last seven of those years, I went into three different state prisons not too far from where I live. The Lord had called me into this ministry supernaturally, and later He called me out supernaturally. I was completely unqualified for this ministry. Child of God, the Lord isn't looking for the qualified, but only for someone willing to do what He asks of them.

One of the greatest lessons I learned while serving in prison was that you cannot put an infinite God in a finite box. As hard as you try to contain God, He will not be contained by man.

Here's a story about one of many lessons the Lord gave me while serving in the prisons:

It was a surreal day, being the last time I would be preaching in prison. I was covering a Sunday service for the state prison chaplain, and I was scheduled to preach in a high-security unit at the prison complex. I'd prepared my last message, making sure I had everything ready. We should always be prepared, but never be so set in our plans that we don't leave room for God's plans.

I was just outside the prison, praying that the Lord would help me to love the chaplain's clerk who would be at this service. Every prison yard has a clerk who's an inmate serving the chaplain of that prison yard. This particular clerk would often treat me poorly, speaking down to me in front of the men during services when I'd been there before. His pride ruled his ministry. But it was my heart I needed to have changed. No matter who is coming against us, we need to first pray for the Lord to change us.

Never think ministry is easy. Ministry is anything but easy. There is much flesh in the ministry that hinders the Holy Spirit. We must pray past the limits of man that we could be serving the kingdom of God. The greatest obstacle you face in ministry is yourself. Seek how God might change you, and let Him worry about everyone else.

The greatest obstacle you face in ministry is yourself.

I went into the prison unit and sat at the back in the chaplain's chair. The men were brought into the chapel, and the correctional officers locked them inside with me. The chaplain's clerk began with worship, and then instead of calling me up to preach as he was supposed to do, he gave his own message using up almost all the service time. I could feel the spirit of pride upon him. There's no greater accomplice to Satan in the church than the pride of man.

His message was brilliant by man's standards. It followed a well-organized outline and stepped through a studied analysis of many Scriptures. He quoted famous men. He gave analogies to make his points stronger. I was impressed with his intellect and oratory skills. But I felt no Holy Spirit. You can always tell when a message is merely from the intellect of man, because your inner spirit isn't moved.

When he finished, he sat down in the front row. He turned and looked back at me with eyes that said, "Top that." I felt sorry for him. The flesh always divides. "These are sensual persons, who cause divisions, not having the Spirit" (Jude 1:19).

We have too much competition in ministry when instead there should be a unity in the Spirit. All of us are only lowly servants to our mighty God. "For I say, through the grace given to me, to everyone who is among you, not to think of himself more highly than he ought to think" (Romans 12:3).

There I was, ready to give my last message in prison. I had one all prepared, but then I heard the Holy Spirit tell me to put it down. Oh, how many times have I heard this before! Child of God, you cannot be led by the Holy Spirit and always hang onto your own plans. I'm quite sure I have dozens of messages either never given or given only in part because I've yielded to the leading of the Holy Spirit. Be willing to yield in your ministering, and it's there that the Holy Spirit can pour through you.

I walked up front without my notes or any idea of what I might say. If you have the Holy Spirit, you never have to worry about what you're going to say. Jesus promised us, "The Holy Spirit will teach you in that very hour what you ought to say" (Luke 12:12). Do you believe the words Jesus spoke? I do. If you would simply believe in the Word, your faith would be unstoppable.

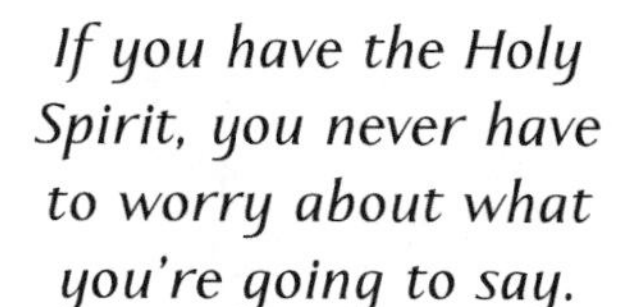
If you have the Holy Spirit, you never have to worry about what you're going to say.

I don't remember the message I gave. I can tell you it was very short. Child of God, the Holy Spirit doesn't need a long message, because every word of the Spirit is piercing into the soul. We need more Holy Spirit messages if we're to have more of the power of the Holy Spirit in our churches. Never think you aren't capable, because it's not about you—and that's the point.

If you want to be led by the Holy Spirit, you must stop limiting how He might lead you. Philip was in the midst of a great revival, saving and healing many in Samaria, but the Holy Spirit called him out to the desert to minister to one. "Then the Spirit said to Philip, 'Go near and overtake this chariot'" (Acts 8:29).

The Holy Spirit cannot lead you unless you're willing to follow.

The Holy Spirit cannot lead you unless you're willing to follow. "Teach me to do your will, because you are my God; let your good Spirit guide me on ground that is level" (Psalm 143:10 CJB).

You cannot follow the Spirit unless you're walking in the Spirit. "I say then: Walk in the Spirit, and you shall not fulfill the lust of the flesh" (Galatians 5:16).

At the beginning of this service, the Lord had revealed to me the man who would get saved that day. For years in my preaching, I had this precious knowing of who would get saved in the service, and it never failed. Man may fail you, but the Lord never will. Concerning the Holy Spirit, Jesus promised that "whatever He hears He will speak; and He will tell you things to come" (John 16:13). Do you believe the Word? Dare to believe, and your life will never be the same.

After my short message, there was no more time left for an altar call. But I knew that the Lord would make a way. We worry only when we don't trust Him. I started doing the altar call, and one by one, the men came forward. After each one came up, I would just pray again for the next one, since the one who I'd been shown would be saved that day was not getting up. Learn to be more stubborn than the devils working against you.

Friends, I want you to know that the Lord gave a great blessing upon my last service in prison. The man who He had showed me would get saved was the last one who came up. The Lord knew I would keep praying until that man came forward. Every man in the service came forward to either get saved or recommit their life to the Lord! "To Him who is able to do exceedingly abundantly above all that we ask or think, according to the power that works in us" (Ephesians 3:20). The Holy Spirit is the power that works in us.

Nobody filled by the Spirit is without the power of the Spirit.

Stop underestimating what an extraordinary God can do through an ordinary person. Dare to be that person.

When they were all up at the front, I looked to the clerk who had taunted me to top his message. Friends, make no mistake about it: I did not top that man's message. But I want you to know, the Holy Spirit did. I asked this clerk to come up and lead the men through the prayer of salvation. Sometimes the greatest lesson you can give someone who has offended you is to simply love them in return.

Stop underestimating what an extraordinary God can do through an ordinary person.

The correctional officers were still not coming, and we were way over our time. Wouldn't you know, I also had time to individually speak a prophetic word into each of these men's lives. It's a precious thing when we can say, as King David said in his last words, "The Spirit of the Lord spoke by me, and His word was on my tongue" (2 Samuel 23:2). It's the most beautiful thing when the Holy Spirit gets hold of a service.

Stop thinking you need to be something. You need to be nothing. It's not by your abilities, but by His. "It is not by force nor by strength, but by My Spirit, says the LORD of Heaven's Armies" (Zechariah 4:6 NLT).

Stop thinking that God cannot use you, and then watch Him use you. Your only qualification is that you're foolish, and be sure that you are. "But God has chosen the foolish things of the world to put to shame the wise" (1 Corinthians 1:27).

God isn't looking for great men and women; rather, He is looking for broken men and women, that He could be great through them. "For thus says the High and Lofty One who inhabits eternity, whose name is Holy: I dwell in the high and holy place, with him who has a contrite and humble spirit" (Isaiah 57:15).

It doesn't matter where God sends me or where He sends you, but only that we follow the leading of the Holy Spirit.

That was many years ago, and I haven't preached in a prison since then. God called me out of that ministry, and I was obedient. Not my will, but His. Perhaps God will bless me to go back inside a prison again someday. It doesn't matter where God sends me or where He sends you, but only that we follow the leading of the Holy Spirit. I hope you do. You'll never go wrong being led by the Holy Spirit.

A Prayer for Being Led by the Holy Spirit

* *Father God, forgive me in however I've tried in my prayers or my words to others to limit or contain all that You might do. Give me a greater knowledge of how infinitely great You are.*

* *Lord Jesus, help me to realize how indescribable You are, that all things were made by You and for You. This is beyond what my mind can grasp. Help me to grasp more of Your majesty.*

* *Holy Spirit, lead me with such clarity and purpose that I won't miss the plans You have for me. Help me to be sensitive to Your precious leadings in my life.*

Spiritual Guide

* Learn to fear God in the right way—not that He would hurt you wrongly, but that He might hurt you rightly. God never hurts you to destroy you, but to restore you. "Teach me Your way, O LORD; I will walk in Your truth; unite my heart to fear Your name" (Psalm 86:11).

* Be willing to follow the leading of the Holy Spirit no matter the cost. "And see, now I go bound in the spirit to Jerusalem, not knowing the things that will happen to me there" (Acts 20:22).

* Be determined to love your enemies so that the Lord could then minister to them through you. Jesus taught, "But love your enemies, do good, and lend, hoping for nothing in return; and your reward will be great, and you will be sons of the Most High" (Luke 6:35).

10
Knowing the Holy Spirit

You don't need a program—you need the Holy Spirit.

"Or do you not know that your body is the temple of the Holy Spirit who is in you, whom you have from God" (1 Corinthians 6:19).

When I came to Christ, I struggled for years to grow stronger in my faith. I joined programs and read books. I strived as hard as anyone could strive. But always I would end up failing or flatlining, and never reaching the heights in my faith I longed for.

I thought I needed to be good to gain the Holy Spirit, but I discovered that I needed to gain the Holy Spirit to be good. It's by Christ alone that you're saved, and it's by the Holy Spirit alone that you can be changed. Try as you might, only the Holy Spirit can change you. Until you have the Holy Spirit reigning in you, your faith will be limited by the power of you.

There are many things we must learn in our faith, but being transformed and empowered by the Holy Spirit is the catapult upon which your faith will reach for the heavens. I pray you would come to know the Holy Spirit as your Friend, your Teacher, and your Helper, so that your life is never the same again.

I prayed for a word to write about the Holy Spirit, and below is the first half of what poured into me and onto paper in just a few minutes. (I added verses to go along with it afterward; the Spirit of God is never contrary to the Word of God.)

Try reading without the verses first; that's how I first heard it. Discern for yourself whatever you read from me or from anyone else (nobody has it all right, except God alone).

You don't need another program. You need the Holy Spirit.

You don't need another book. You need the Holy Spirit.

Try as you might to be stronger in your faith apart from the Holy Spirit, you are the limit of you.

The Spirit of God is never contrary to the Word of God.

We have one God. "Hear, O Israel: The LORD our God, the LORD is one!" (Deuteronomy 6:4).

Our God is three in Person. Jesus taught, "Go therefore and make disciples of all the nations, baptizing them in the name of the Father and of the Son and of the Holy Spirit" (Matthew 28:19).

There is God the Father. There is God the Son. There is God the Holy Spirit. "For there are three that bear witness in heaven: the Father, the Word [Jesus], and the Holy Spirit; and these three are one" (1 John 5:7).

No one can come to the Father but through the Son. "Jesus said to him, 'I am the way, the truth, and the life. No one comes to the Father except through Me'" (John 14:6).

No one can come to the Son but by the Holy Spirit. It is the Father that draws you to the Son by the Holy Spirit. Jesus taught, "No one can come to Me unless the Father who sent Me draws him" (John 6:44).

We cannot fully comprehend the Triune God. The Trinity of three Persons as one God cannot be fully grasped by the finite mind of a simple man or woman here on earth.

God is bigger than your imagination, and He is bigger than your understanding. "For as the heavens are higher than the earth, so are My ways higher than your ways, and My thoughts than your thoughts" (Isaiah 55:9).

We learn about the Father through the Son. Jesus taught, "Nor does anyone know the Father except the Son, and the one to whom the Son wills to reveal Him" (Matthew 11:27).

We learn about the Son through the Holy Spirit. Jesus taught, "The Holy Spirit—he will teach you everything and will remind you of everything I have told you" (John 14:26 NLT).

The Son is no less than the Father.

The Holy Spirit is no less than the Son.

Each Person of the Trinity is God, so no part of the Trinity is less than God.

The Father stands above all creation. "No one has seen God at any time" (John 1:18).

The Son entered into creation to restore mankind to the Father. "For it pleased the Father that in Him [Jesus] all the fullness [of God] should dwell, and by Him [Jesus] to reconcile all things to Himself [The Father], by Him [Jesus], whether things on earth or things in heaven, having made peace through the blood of His cross" (Colossians 1:19-20).

The Son returned to the Father, and the Father then sent the Holy Spirit to mankind. "This Helper is the Holy Spirit that the Father will send in My name" (John 14:26 ERV).

The Son came and saved us from our sin by His blood. "You were not redeemed with corruptible things...but with the precious blood of Christ" (1 Peter 1:18-19).

The Holy Spirit came to give us power over sin. "But you shall receive power when the Holy Spirit has come upon you" (Acts 1:8).

The Son serves the Father.

The Holy Spirit serves the Son.

We do not dishonor the Father or the Son when we rely on the Holy Spirit; rather we honor them, because the Holy Spirit was sent that we might know them and serve them.

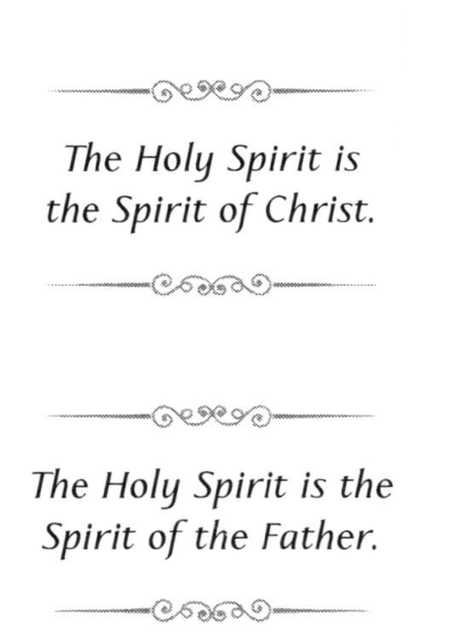
The Holy Spirit is the Spirit of Christ.
The Holy Spirit is the Spirit of the Father.

The Holy Spirit is the Spirit of Christ. "Now if anyone does not have the Spirit of Christ, he is not His" (Romans 8:9). "And because you are sons, God has sent forth the Spirit of His Son into your hearts" (Galatians 4:6).

The Holy Spirit is the Spirit of the Father. "But you are not in the flesh but in the Spirit, if indeed the Spirit of God dwells in you" (Romans 8:9). God said, "I will put My Spirit within you" (Ezekiel 36:27).

When Christ said that if we abide in Him, He would abide in us, it was the Spirit of Christ, the Holy Spirit, of whom He was talking about. Jesus taught, "I am the vine, you are the branches. He who abides in Me, and I in him, bears much fruit; for without Me you can do nothing" (John 15:5).

When the prophecy was given that God would dwell with men, it was His Holy Spirit coming into man that fulfilled this prophecy. "I will put My Spirit within you" (Ezekiel 36:27).

The temple of God represented the body of man that would one day become the living temple of the Holy Spirit. "The glory of this latter temple shall be greater than the former, says the LORD of hosts. And in this place I will give peace" (Haggai 2:9). "Or do you not know that your body is the temple of the Holy Spirit who is in you, whom you have from God" (1 Corinthians 6:19).

The Holy Spirit can be your best Friend, Teacher, Counselor, Helper—God in you, Christ in you, a new life in you, a new life for you. Won't you ask the Father to give you a greater presence of His Holy Spirit in you today? Jesus promised, "How much more will your heavenly Father give the Holy Spirit to those who ask Him!" (Luke 11:13).

This was the first half of what I heard (the next half is in the next chapter). I've learned that as we read the Word every day for many years, the Word comes alive in us and through us. The Holy Spirit brings the Word to our remembrance—sometimes word for word, and other times paraphrased and expressed in a new way.

The Holy Spirit will never change the truth of the Word, but He merely brings you greater revelations of the truth that's already there. If you have yet to become immersed in the Word of God, always start there. Many have been deceived by a wrong spirit because they have not had the plumb line of truth with the Word of God by which to test it.

As we must grow over time in the natural, slowly gaining new skills of crawling and walking, so it must be in the spiritual. Don't rush spiritual growth. Get your footing and learn to walk before you run and possibly fall. We live in the age of instant gratification and super-growth schemes. It took God forty years to prepare Moses; stop thinking you can somehow be ready so much faster.

Don't rush spiritual growth.

Too often when we see people who've grown near to the Lord and have a closeness with the Holy Spirit, we don't consider all that they've been through to get there. Child of God, nobody gets that close to God on the mountain without first having walked a long time in the valley. Don't rush your time in the valley; that's exactly where He's preparing you to ascend the mountain.

A Prayer for Knowing the Holy Spirit

- *Father God, help me to know the Holy Spirit with a deeper intimacy and a greater clarity every day. Help me to know the truth by Your Word.*
- *Lord Jesus, thank you for praying to the Father to send the Holy Spirit to live inside me. Help me by the power of the Holy Spirit to have Your life reigning in me.*
- *Holy Spirit, I pray that You would help me to know the Father and to know the Son with deeper intimacy and greater knowledge.*

Spiritual Guide

- Pray with thanksgiving in your heart, giving praises to God. When we praise Him, we're telling Him that we trust Him in everything He does. "Oh, give thanks to the LORD, for He is good! For His mercy endures forever" (Psalm 136:1).
- Pray that the Lord would show you whom you need to forgive. We must be free from a heart of unforgiveness if we're to be filled with the Holy Spirit from our Father who has forgiven us. "And be kind to one another, tenderhearted, forgiving one another, even as God in Christ forgave you" (Ephesians 4:32).
- Learn to pray from the depth of your soul to a God who longs to have you trust Him with your heart and everything you hold within it. "In my distress I called upon the LORD, and cried out to my God; He heard my voice from His temple, and my cry came before Him, even to His ears" (Psalm 18:6).

11 Having the Holy Spirit

The greatest gift of God to you is Himself, in the Holy Spirit.

"The gift of the Holy Spirit had been poured out..." (Acts 10:45).

This is a continuation from what I wrote on "Knowing the Holy Spirit" in the prior chapter.

I'm convinced that in however we fail in our faith, we haven't yet surrendered that part of our life to the Holy Spirit. People have told me that you either have the Holy Spirit or you don't, and that the degree the Holy Spirit reigns in your life cannot be increased. How horribly wrong they are in their natural assessment that leaves themselves spiritually weak.

Child of God, we need to pray for a greater filling of the Holy Spirit in our lives every day. Apart from the Holy Spirit being active in our lives, we'll remain powerless and be only as strong as the meager levels that our broken flesh can muster up. You were meant for something more than that.

There are no limits to what can be done through the life of a saint filled with the Spirit of God.

Child of God, there are no limits to what can be done through the life of a saint filled with the Spirit of God. As you let Him reign in you, the Holy Spirit will do things that you never even imagined He might do. God has an imagination bigger than your imagination. God has a plan bigger than your plan. God has all the resources in heaven at His disposal, and all we must do is welcome the Holy Spirit in our life.

There are people you know and people you'll meet who will be forever grateful and blessed if you let the Spirit of God move through you. What you do today matters for everything that will happen tomorrow. No matter where you find yourself, that's where God can start. Let Him start today.

No matter where you find yourself, that's where God can start.

Give your life to Him, and He will give His life to you, and your life will never be the same again. Child of God, you were meant for something more. Your life can go so much higher. There are two things that will always hinder your ascension spiritually: thinking you can't, or thinking you have no further to go. Both of these are wrong, because you can ascend by His power, and there's an infinite level to which you can ascend. Nobody reaches the top with an infinite God in heaven.

I had prayed for a word to write about the Holy Spirit, and below is the second half of what poured into me and onto paper in just a few minutes. (Try reading it first without the verses; that's how I first heard it.)

The Holy Spirit can teach you all things. Jesus promised that the Holy Spirit "will teach you all things" (John 14:26).

The Holy Spirit can put thoughts in your mind. "The Holy Spirit... [will] bring to your remembrance..." (John 14:26).

The Holy Spirit can give you words to speak. "For the Holy Spirit will teach you in that very hour what you ought to say" (Luke 12:12).

The Holy Spirit can give you revelations. "For prophecy never came by the will of man, but holy men of God spoke as they were moved by the Holy Spirit" (2 Peter 1:21).

The Holy Spirit can reveal Christ to you. "No one can say that Jesus is Lord except by the Holy Spirit" (1 Corinthians 12:3).

The Holy Spirit can reveal the Father to you. "That the God of our Lord Jesus Christ...may give to you the spirit of wisdom and revelation in the knowledge of Him" (Ephesians 1:17).

The Holy Spirit can give you power. "But you shall receive power when the Holy Spirit has come upon you" (Acts 1:8).

The Holy Spirit can give you dreams and visions. "And it shall come to pass afterward that I will pour out My Spirit on all flesh; your sons and your daughters shall prophesy, your old men shall dream dreams, your young men shall see visions" (Joel 2:28).

The Holy Spirit can heal others through you. "To another gifts of healings by the same Spirit" (1 Corinthians 12:9).

The Holy Spirit can give you fruit from a new heart. "But the Holy Spirit produces this kind of fruit in our lives: love, joy, peace, patience, kindness, goodness, faithfulness, gentleness, and self-control" (Galatians 5:22-23 NLT).

The Holy Spirit can give you gifts by which you can serve God. "There are diversities of gifts, but the same Spirit" (1 Corinthians 12:4).

The Holy Spirit can give you a new language in which you can speak to God. "For he who speaks in a tongue does not speak to men but to God, for no one understands him; however, in the spirit he speaks mysteries" (1 Corinthians 14:1-2).

The greatest gift of God to you is Himself, in the Holy Spirit. "Don't you realize that your body is the temple of the Holy Spirit, who lives in you and was given to you by God? You do not belong to yourself, for God bought you with a high price. So you must honor God with your body" (1 Corinthians 6:19-20 NLT).

The greatest gift of God to you is Himself, in the Holy Spirit.

Don't chase anything except God. "But from there you will seek the LORD your God, and you will find Him if you seek Him with all your heart and with all your soul" (Deuteronomy 4:29).

Don't yield to anything except God. "Yield yourselves to the LORD" (2 Chronicles 30:8).

Don't desire anything more than God. "You shall love the Lord your God with all your heart, with all your soul, and with all your mind" (Matthew 22:37).

Let the Holy Spirit be everything to you, and He will be everything in you and through you. "Now He who has prepared us for this very thing is God, who also has given us the Spirit as a guarantee" (2 Corinthians 5:5).

Your talent cannot gain the Holy Spirit. "The gift of the Holy Spirit" (Acts 10:45).

Your intellect and money are worthless to the Holy Spirit. "Your heavenly Father [will] give the Holy Spirit to those who ask Him" (Luke 11:13).

You cannot take the Holy Spirit, but only receive Him. "You shall receive the gift of the Holy Spirit" (Acts 2:38).

Your surrender leads to your victory. "Therefore submit to God. Resist the devil and he will flee from you" (James 4:7).

Your willingness leads to His manifestation. "But the manifestation of the Spirit is given to each one for the profit of all" (1 Corinthians 12:7).

Your faith is greater than anything else you have. "For whatever is born of God overcomes the world. And this is the victory that has overcome the world—our faith" (1 John 5:4).

There is nothing on this earth besides the Holy Spirit that can transform you into something new. "But we all, with unveiled face, beholding as in a mirror the glory of the Lord, are being transformed into the same image from glory to glory, just as by the Spirit of the Lord" (2 Corinthians 3:18).

Stop trying so hard, and just let the Holy Spirit have His way in you.

The Holy Spirit is a match made in heaven for you. Won't you pray to the Father and to the Son that you would come to know the Holy Spirit more and more in your life each day?

Stop trying so hard, and just let the Holy Spirit have His way in you.

This was the end of what I received that day. Child of God, it's such a privilege for us that God has sent His Spirit to live within us. We can reach so much higher, if we would only kneel so much lower. The God who created us speaks to us in His Word, through His creation, and by His Spirit living within us. We must learn to listen, to be so still that we can hear His whisper.

There's so much more that the Holy Spirit can do in our lives. We read the Word, but often we miss the wonder of what God is telling us. Here are some precious truths of what the Holy Spirit can do in your life:

We can reach so much higher, if we would only kneel so much lower.

The Holy Spirit can supernaturally transport you. "Now when they came up out of the water, the Spirit of the Lord caught Philip away" (Acts 8:39).

When the Holy Spirit is upon you, nothing will be impossible any longer. "And the Spirit of the LORD came mightily upon him, and he tore the lion apart as one would have torn apart a young goat, though he had nothing in his hand" (Judges 14:6).

The Holy Spirit can bring you revelations of what can happen in the future. "And it had been revealed to him by the Holy Spirit that he would not see death before he had seen the Lord's Christ" (Luke 2:26).

The Holy Spirit can make and break your travel plans. "After they had come to Mysia, they tried to go into Bithynia, but the Spirit did not permit them" (Acts 16:7).

Never doubt what the Holy Spirit can do in your life, if you will only believe.

Never doubt what the Holy Spirit can do in your life, if you will only believe.

I've had the honor of meeting many anointed servants in my faith journey, from the precious men and women I met while in prison ministry, to special souls I've met while traveling to different places. Some people I meet are far along and have such a rich and deep experience with the Holy Spirit. I'm inspired by such people. Their relationship with God moves me to desire the same. We all need to be inspired. We all should seek to inspire others. We need each other. Someone needs you.

We're all on a journey, wherever we may be along the path. Don't be discouraged with where you are, but be inspired to press on and reach for something more. The beauty is this: Our spiritual growth is not dependent on our abilities, but His. Child of God, He is able. I may tell you in a hundred different ways about how you need to just surrender to Him, and my prayer is that at least one of the ways will move you to get down onto your knees and finally do so.

My prayer is to move even one person closer to God. Will you be that one?

A Prayer for Having the Holy Spirit

* *Father God, I pray that You would pour into me the fullness of the Holy Spirit and the Spirit of wisdom and revelation in the knowledge of You.*
* *Lord Jesus, I pray that by the Holy Spirit I would gain the remembrance of the words You spoke, that having Your Words in me would help me have Your life reign in me.*
* *Holy Spirit, I pray that I would become so spiritually sensitive that I would hear You clearly, and follow You diligently, and learn from You carefully.*

Spiritual Guide

* Consider starting a daily journal by which you could make declarations in your life to the Father, the Son, and the Holy Spirit. It's not enough to think about it; write it down. Once you write it down, it's a plan. We'll do what we determine to do. "Commit your way to the Lord, trust also in Him, and He shall bring it to pass" (Psalm 37:5).

- Declare for yourself what you want to have. Write out the character traits of God that you want to have the Spirit of God start to form in you. If you want to be different, then say it out loud. "Commit your works to the LORD, and your thoughts will be established" (Proverbs 16:3).

- Be patient with God, knowing He's being patient with you. He'll never give you anything more than you're ready for. "And being assembled together with them, He commanded them not to depart from Jerusalem, but to wait for the Promise of the Father [the Holy Spirit], 'which,' He said, 'you have heard from Me'" (Acts 1:4).

12 Spiritual Revelations

You don't gain faith through revelation, but revelation through faith.

"I pray that the Father of glory, the God of our Lord Jesus Christ, would impart to you the riches of the Spirit of wisdom and the Spirit of revelation to know Him [the Father] through your deepening intimacy with Him" (Ephesians 1:17 TPT).

I remember the first day that I heard the Lord. It shook me at my foundation. I didn't know we could hear the Holy Spirit. After that first time, there was a span of many months before I heard His voice again. I continued to hear the Holy Spirit from time to time over several years, but then one day the floodgates opened, and the river began to flow. It hasn't stopped flowing ever since that day.

Your experience with the Lord will be just as unique, as you are a unique design of His. Don't try to find a pattern for how God might operate; just be willing to hear Him when He would speak to you. Be immersed in the Word of God so that you can discern the voice of God. We come to know the heart of God through the Word of God. We must keep the Word as our foundation.

We come to know the heart of God through the Word of God.

We're most blessed if we gain in revelations from the Holy Spirit, so that we know the Word of God deeper as revealed by the Spirit of God into our hearts. My greatest hope is that more believers would believe that the God who inspired the Bible has sent His Spirit so we can better understand it. In times past, all they had was the letter of the law, but we now have the Spirit of the law living within us. I pray that you would walk in revelations from the Holy Spirit.

His power is not dependent on yours, but yours on His.

The greatest barrier to the revelation of truth is the lie that you firmly hold onto.

You will not hear in the spiritual if you listen only in the natural.

It is not by our effort but by His that we can hear the Holy Spirit. The Lord God told Jeremiah, "I will cause you to hear My words" (Jeremiah 18:2).

The greatest barrier to the revelation of truth is the lie that you firmly hold onto.

The spiritually unborn cannot yet hear spiritually. See to it that they are first born in the Spirit, then you can teach them to listen as they mature.

Child of God, learn how to rest in God. Be still before God. Be quiet before God. We have too many people trying to be strong enough to get to God, when they need to be weak before God. If you're still working,

God is still waiting. When once you finally give up and give in, you'll kick yourself in the behind for being so stubborn and making it so hard.

You will never get closer to God walking on natural paths. You cannot learn spiritual truths with natural study methods.

You cannot climb spiritual mountains, but only be lifted to them. The harder you try, the prouder you are.

It's the pride of man that says he must do the work. That's why the Lord cannot do a work through a proud man.

Child of God, my greatest hope is that wherever you are in your faith, the Lord would take you higher. Don't let your imagination limit what the Lord might do. Whether it be a burning bush or an angel of the Lord in your dream, keep yourself ready, keep yourself open, that He could speak to you.

Listening Prayers

Try praying with your ears wide open.

You never have to pray for the Holy Spirit to speak to you, but only that you would have ears to hear Him. "He who has an ear, let him hear what the Spirit says" (Revelation 2:29).

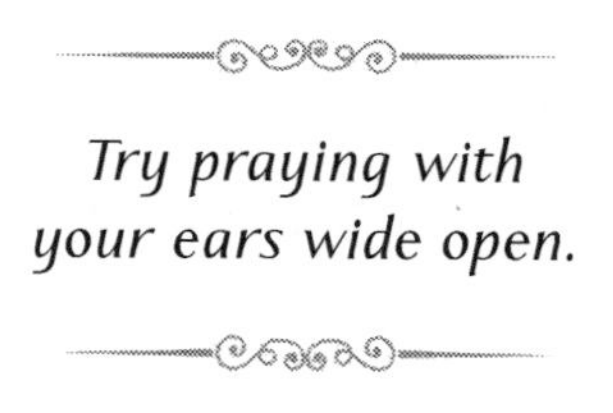
Try praying with
your ears wide open.

Our problem with communicating is not that we don't talk to Him; our problem is that we don't listen to Him. You cannot hear with your mouth wide open.

One of the greatest obstacles of the Holy Spirit speaking to you is that you don't have ears by which you can hear Him. These aren't the natural ears on the side of your head, but the spiritual ears of your heart. We need our heart softened to God, believing in what He can do. Get by yourself and pray for Him to speak to you—even if only one word. What is the word He has for you today?

If you don't believe the Lord will speak to you, then you won't listen. Or you don't listen because you know what He would tell you.

It's never a question of whether the Lord will speak to you, but whether you will hear Him. "Your ears shall hear a word behind you, saying, 'This is the way, walk in it'" (Isaiah 30:21).

It's never a question of whether the Lord will speak to you, but whether you will hear Him.

You need to have holy ears so that you can hear a Holy Spirit.

God holds back until you're ready. "Yet the LORD has not given you a heart to perceive and eyes to see and ears to hear, to this very day" (Deuteronomy 29:4). He waits until we're ready. God is Spirit, His Word is Spirit, so we must listen in the Spirit. Quiet your mind that you would hear His voice.

There are many want-to-be prophets in our world. Don't be one of those. Be willing to be nothing, and be careful in all you do. We will be judged; let us never act as if we won't. We must be careful in how we preach on the Word of God, and even more careful on any word we believe that He has given us.

Let the Lord work on you, and perhaps later He will speak through you to another. But never go into that lightly, because if we prophesy falsely, we're slandering a holy and mighty God. Seek revelation to change you. Let Him change you in every way that you're wrong. Be willing to be wrong that He can make you right.

You don't gain revelation; it must be given to you.

Be willing to be wrong that He can make you right.

The Lord cannot reveal a new thing until you first have eyes from which you can see. Pray to the Lord, "Open my eyes that I may see wonderful things in your law" (Psalm 119:18).

Spiritual revelation cannot be mined using the tools of man. So long as you rely solely upon man, the Spirit of God will not help you. "These things we also speak, not in words which man's wisdom teaches but which the Holy Spirit teaches, comparing spiritual things with spiritual. But the natural man does not receive the things of the Spirit of God, for they are foolishness to him; nor can he know them, because they are spiritually discerned" (1 Corinthians 2:13-14).

You won't gain more revelation of truth until you start living the truth already revealed to you. "The secret things belong to the LORD our God, but those things which are revealed belong to us and to our children forever, that we may do all the words of this law" (Deuteronomy 29:29).

With the Word there is light, and in the light, there is revelation. "Your word is a lamp to my feet and a light to my path" (Psalm 119:105).

I'm always encouraging people to grow in their spiritual life. But I'm always cautioning people as they do so. This is because I've seen both sides—those who don't grow in the Spirit, and those who do so without caution and go after the wrong spirit. Just fall before Christ the Lord, pray always, stay humble, stay in the Word of God, and trust in Him to help you every step of the way.

I'm also encouraging churches to be open to the revelations from the Spirit of God. I admire the caution and the concern. We must stay in the Word that we would be on solid and good ground. But we must not ignore those parts of the Word that speak of the power and the purpose of the Holy Spirit for the church in our day.

Many fear false prophets so much that they reject true prophets. Jesus said to test prophets, not reject them.

The Holy Spirit will not pour out revelation into closed minds.

Don't reveal less so your teaching is safer, but reveal more that your teaching is

The Holy Spirit will not pour out revelation into closed minds.

more effective. Jesus never limited His teaching by what they would receive, and neither should you.

The secret to revelation in God's Word is that it cannot be found, but only revealed.

Never search for revelation only to teach, but also to learn. Then teach only what you are willing to live. If you don't live the truth, you'll be preaching from the platform of a lie.

Revelation is not always a new truth, but a hidden truth revealed. Revelation is not just what will be, but what already is.

The more we fear Him, the more He will reveal. "The secret of the LORD is with those who fear Him, and He will show them His covenant" (Psalm 25:14).

A Prayer to Gain Revelations from the Holy Spirit

* *Father God, help me to know You deeper, that You are always in agreement with Your Word and Your Spirit. Teach me by Your Spirit to live and to minister to others in truth.*

* *Lord Jesus, I pray that the Holy Spirit will bring to my remembrance throughout each day the Word that You have spoken. Help me, Lord, to not only hear the Word but also to walk in it.*

* *Holy Spirit, help me to discern Your voice over my own. Help me not to be clever but to be open in my mind to hear from You. Help me understand that in myself I could never think of the things You have to give me.*

Spiritual Guide

* Be patient in waiting for a word from the Lord. "I wait for the LORD, my soul waits, and in His word I do hope" (Psalm 130:5).

* Be willing to hear a word you may not want to hear. "My son, do not despise the chastening of the Lord, nor be discouraged when you are rebuked by Him; for whom the Lord loves He chastens, and scourges every son whom He receives" (Hebrews 12:5-6).

* Get into His will and then pray confidently. "Now this is the confidence that we have in Him, that if we ask anything according to His will, He hears us" (1 John 5:14).

13 Guided by the Holy Spirit

Just as you can talk to God, be sure that He can talk to you.

The Lord said, "With your ears you will hear a word from behind you: This is the way; stay on it, whether you go to the right or the left" (Isaiah 30:21 CJB).

Early on in my faith, I didn't know much. I just believed. Not much has changed. I think the problem nowadays is that too many Christians know much but believe little.

One night many years ago, before I had started doing prison ministry, I was riding my motorcycle to church for a Bible study. I was riding down a four-lane street with hardly any traffic going in either direction. Suddenly I heard the voice of the Holy Spirit telling me to stop. It made no sense, but I slammed on my brakes and came to a stop right there in the middle of the street. At that moment, a car pulled out very fast, crossing over just inches in front of me. The driver was looking the other way. This car would have plowed right into me had I not stopped. I thanked God and then rode on to church.

At the end of the Bible study, we were all talking, and I told the others there about what had happened earlier that night. They looked at me in shock that I'd heard the Holy Spirit. I didn't know I wasn't supposed to. I was just a young Christian, and I thought every Christian heard the Holy Spirit. Now I know that not every Christian does hear the Holy Spirit, but I know that every Christian can.

Holy Spirit Speaking

I want you to know that you can hear the Holy Spirit. It is not by our effort, but by His that we can hear Him. The Lord said, "I will cause thee to hear my words" (Jeremiah 18:2 KJV).

The Father only spoke to some, but the Holy Spirit speaks to all believers. The problem we have with most believers is that they don't believe. Jesus said, "If you can believe, all things are possible to him who believes" (Mark 9:23).

The problem we have with most believers is that they don't believe.

Stop thinking you are not worthy enough to hear the Holy Spirit. Only the devil would tell you that. You are a son or daughter of the Father, and He has sent the Holy Spirit to help you. Believe the Word of God more than the lies of the devil. "I will be a Father to you, and you shall be My sons and daughters, says the Lord Almighty" (2 Corinthians 6:18).

Never worry what people might think of you as you tell them your experiences with the Holy Spirit. Tell them anyway. Let us tell the truth, so that it can edify those willing to receive it. "Even so you, since you are zealous for spiritual gifts, let it be for the edification of the church that you seek to excel" (1 Corinthians 14:12).

God is not mute. The only ones who preach that He doesn't talk are those who do not hear Him. They preach to the level they're at, to justify their experience that there is no more. But there is more. Keep pressing in. God's Word warns us that "in the last days" there will be those "having a form of godliness but denying its power. And from such people turn away!" (2 Timothy 3:1,5).

Peter preached that the prophetic words from the prophet Joel had already been fulfilled at Pentecost: "And it shall come to pass in the last days, says God, that I will pour out of My Spirit on all flesh; your sons and your daughters shall prophesy" (Acts 2:17). *To this day, the Holy Spirit still flows.*

We are meant to have a holy communion with the Holy Spirit. "The grace of the Lord Jesus Christ, and the love of God, and the communion of the Holy Spirit be with you all. Amen" (2 Corinthians 13:14).

We are meant to have a holy communion with the Holy Spirit.

Many of those who hear the Holy Spirit don't realize that what they hear is from Him. Those of us in Christ are being led by the Spirit of God. We get the nudge, the word, the direction, but too often we ascribe it to our own clever heart. Child of God, we aren't that good to gain the direction out of our own heart. "The heart is deceitful above all things, and desperately wicked; who can know it?" (Jeremiah 17:9).

We need to learn to discern the voice of the Holy Spirit. We need to make sure that our own selfish voice isn't leading us to what our flesh wants. We need to understand the demonic voice that would lead us away from God. Always test the motives in the voice, keep everything in prayer, and whenever you're unsure, wait on the Lord.

There are some things for which I've asked the Lord's direction, and I went for months without His leading. Whenever I don't have a divine leading, I follow natural lines until I do. For example, I prayed about whether I should leave a job, and at first I didn't get an answer. So until I got an answer, I followed natural lines, working hard and being committed in all that I was doing. Months later, the Lord led me on exactly what to do, and I was blessed because of my obedience. Don't rush the Lord, and don't plagiarize the voice of the Holy Spirit with your own voice that always gives you what you desire.

We're all such impatient creatures. Sometimes the Lord will make you wait to see if you will. Be faithful in your waiting. It's in waiting that we're being prepared for bigger things that lie ahead. Show Him you can be trusted to wait for Him.

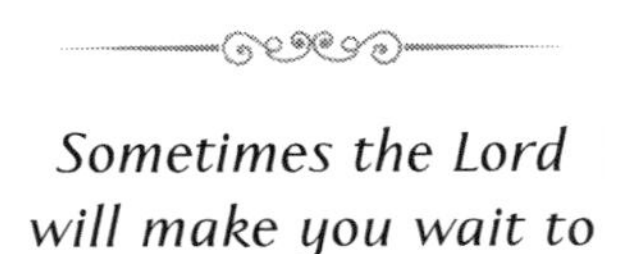

Sometimes the Lord will make you wait to see if you will.

Holy Spirit Leading

Spiritual truth requires a spiritual teacher, and that teacher is found only in the Holy Spirit. The Lord Jesus said, "The Comforter, which is the Holy Ghost, whom the Father will send in My name, He shall teach you all things" (John 14:26 KJV).

Pray that the Holy Spirit will bring you the revelations He alone is qualified to give you.

In our natural, we need the Holy Spirit as our interpreter to the spiritual. God is Spirit, His law is Spirit, so we must learn in the Spirit. "For we know that the law is spiritual" (Romans 7:14).

The Holy Spirit will never say anything that doesn't line up with the Word of God, and often the Word is exactly what He'll give you. If you don't know the Word, then go and start learning it.

Learning to discern the voice of the Holy Spirit is a blessed journey. Find a mature believer to be your mentor. You'll find that a mature believer is very reserved in their walk with God. Nobody gets near to God and stands proudly any longer. The first step to being humble before God is being humble before man. Find a mentor with which to humble yourself. "Humble yourselves in the sight of the Lord, and He will lift you up" (James 4:10).

Never seek a word from the Holy Spirit to be known by men, but only to be known by God. Never think something is too small to seek the leading of the Holy Spirit. Learn to let the Holy Spirit show you where you're wrong. In the conviction of the Holy Spirit, the Father is preparing you. So long as you're being rebuked, you're on the right path.

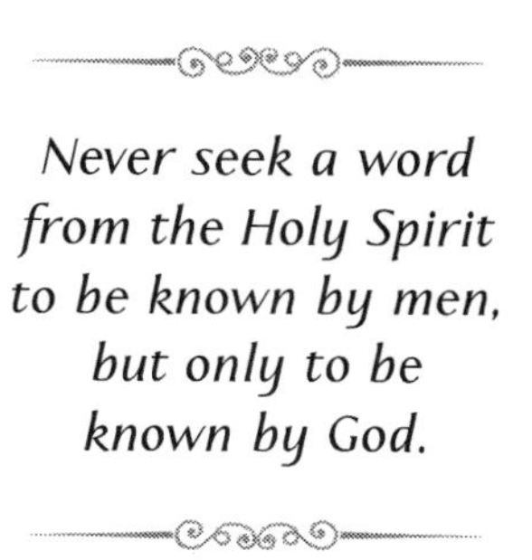
Never seek a word from the Holy Spirit to be known by men, but only to be known by God.

Holy Spirit Conversations

The voice of the Holy Spirit will not come as a natural voice. You need your spiritual ears to hear in the Spirit realm.

If you're born again in the Spirit, you have spiritual senses. These senses may be dulled by the natural, but you have them. Like your physical body, you must learn to grow in the Spirit and use these senses. You must learn to discern His voice. This will take more than a day or two. Figure on it taking a lifetime.

Your problem is not that the Holy Spirit won't listen to you, but that you won't listen to Him. Pray with your ears. Ask for but a single word, and be still until you hear Him.

If you want to hear the Holy Spirit, you must first be filled with the Holy Spirit. "While Peter was still speaking these words, the Holy Spirit fell upon all those who heard the word" (Acts 10:44).

Determine in your heart not to end a prayer until you hear Him.

If you're in sin, get out of your sin. Sin will muffle your ears. It's like running from the Lord and wondering why you cannot hear His whisper. Repent from your sin, confess your sin, turn to Him, draw near to Him, and then you'll be able to hear His whispers to you.

So long as the things of this world are enough for you, that's all you'll get.

You can have a greater filling of the Holy Spirit in your life every day. You'll reach for what you want. Reach for it. The Holy Spirit is never the problem in your spiritual dryness. To be filled with the Holy Spirit, you don't need man's programs or processes, but only a willing heart. The way we'll be filled with more of the Holy Spirit is in our determination to not be satisfied with anything else. So long as the things of this world are enough for you, that's all you'll get.

Increasing in the Holy Spirit

Let your wilderness grow you. Your life is the classroom, and your circumstances are the lesson. "Therefore, as the Holy Spirit says: 'Today, if you will hear His voice, do not harden your hearts as in the rebellion, in the day of trial in the wilderness...'" (Hebrews 3:7-8).

If you want to step more into the spiritual, you must be willing to consecrate more from the natural. "As they ministered to the Lord and fasted, the Holy Spirit said, 'Now separate to Me Barnabas and Saul for the work to which I have called them'" (Acts 13:2).

Never underestimate the power gained through the discipline of prayer and fasting.

Never underestimate the power gained through the discipline of prayer and fasting. The fasted life is the Spirit-filled life. There is always a cost for an increase.

Being obedient to the Holy Spirit is the key to getting more. Don't expect the words from the Holy Spirit to always be in long sentences. Sometimes I'll get only a single word. The first time I heard the Holy Spirit, I was faced with something I felt completely unqualified and unable to do. The two words I heard were these: "Trust Me." Those two words changed the course of my life. Be willing to get only one word from the Holy Spirit, and watch what He can do with that.

A Prayer for Being Guided by the Holy Spirit

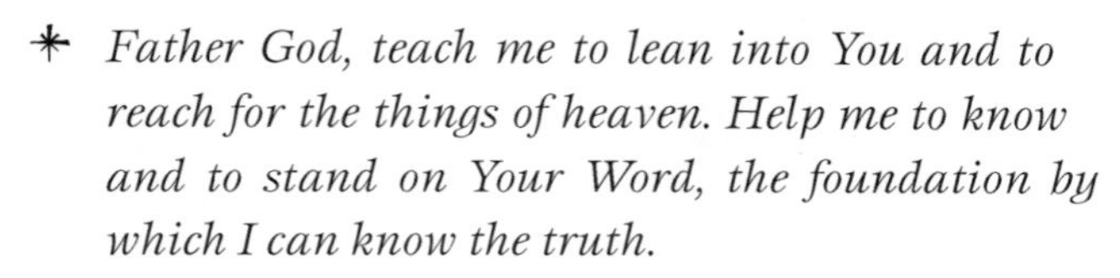

* *Father God, teach me to lean into You and to reach for the things of heaven. Help me to know and to stand on Your Word, the foundation by which I can know the truth.*

* *Lord Jesus, help me to remain so humble that I can hear the Holy Spirit and remain meek and humble before You and before men, so that I walk as You want me to.*

* *Holy Spirit, give me clarity so that I know Your voice and hear Your voice clearly. Teach me to discern the evil one and how he would try to deceive me by counterfeiting You.*

Spiritual Guide

* Pray with your ears, learning to ask things from God and then wait for Him to answer. Be willing to listen more than you speak when you're conversing with God. The Lord said, "Call out to me, and I will answer you—I will tell you great things, hidden things of which you are unaware" (Jeremiah 33:3 CJB).

* Pray the promises of God. When you read a promise from God in the Word of God, pray it out loud and affirm it as truth over your life. "In the same way, My words leave My mouth, and they don't come back without results. My words make the things happen that I want to happen. They succeed in doing what I send them to do" (Isaiah 55:11 ERV).

* Live a simple and unobstructed life. Start to unclutter yourself from the world. Even if you do this in but one room where you live, you'll be blessed in the simplicity. "Make it your ambition to live quietly, to mind your own business and to earn your living by your own efforts—just as we told you" (1 Thessalonians 4:11 CJB).

14

Walking in the Spirit

The most brilliant minds on earth debate what walking in the Spirit means, but it is in the faith like a child that the believer simply does it.

"But I say, walk by the Spirit, and you will not carry out the desire of the flesh" (Galatians 5:16 NASB).

When God called me to serve inside prisons, I was extremely reluctant because of my great difficulty in being around people. I have a sensory condition that often hurts me beyond measure. It's a cruel condition in which normal sensory inputs are abnormally painful. People with autism have this sensory error as one part of their condition.

Everyone carries some difficulty, including you. Yours may be different from mine, but God has allowed it for a reason. Know that God can help you with whatever burden you're carrying. Know that God can bring good from anything bad that may be upon you.

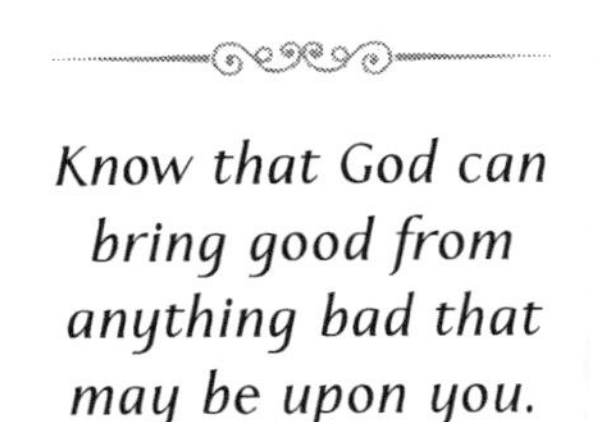
Know that God can bring good from anything bad that may be upon you.

Because of my condition, I've spent my life as a loner. Because of this I wasn't good at being around people. Being called to minister inside prisons seemed like something impossible for me to do. I was angry at God for even asking me to do this, since He's the one who allowed me to be so broken. But now I know that God doesn't need our abilities to use us; He can do more in our weakness than in our strength. I'm still carrying this condition, but thank God, He is carrying me.

It was in this position of helplessness that I learned to rely solely upon the Holy Spirit. I desperately prayed for the Holy Spirit to help me as I was teaching and preaching in prisons. For the first few years I wasn't effective, because I wasn't yet fully surrendered to the Spirit of God. But as I pressed in more, I fell more into the hands of a powerful God. This is not to my credit but to my shame, since it took me so long to get there.

As I continued to serve God, I started experiencing a greater presence of the Holy Spirit upon me. It had nothing to do with my abilities, but only my weaknesses. I thank God He made me so weak. I pray that you would see the great blessings in whatever weaknesses you have in your life. God designs weaknesses in us that His glory could shine through us. What I once saw as curse on my life turned out to be a blessing in disguise. But we must seek the Lord so that He can show us His purposes in our weaknesses.

You Can Walk in the Spirit

The Word of God never tells us to do what we cannot do. His Word commands us, "Walk in the Spirit" (Galatians 5:16). You can walk in the Spirit. If you want to walk in the Spirit, you must be filled with the Spirit. This filling doesn't come by the effort of man, but by the grace of God. It takes no effort of your own, but only a willingness to be surrendered to the Holy Spirit in your life.

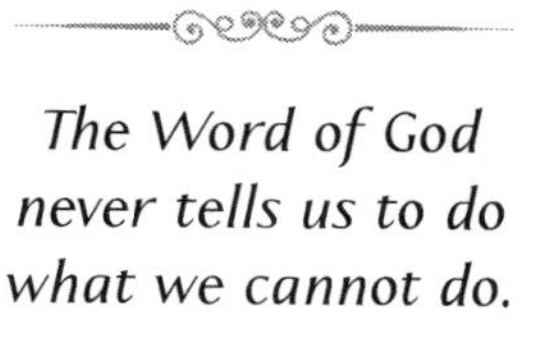

The Word of God never tells us to do what we cannot do.

When you read the Word of God, learn to believe it. Start to take hold of the promises. Nothing was written in error or above you, but God can bring about all these things in you. It's only your strength that gets in God's way, and your weakness that will let Him in.

Learning to walk in the Spirit is not a matter of salvation, but sanctification. This is not a matter of making it into heaven, but it will determine your position once you get there.

Walking in the Spirit is for all, not just some. "The evidence of the Spirit's presence is given to each person for the common good of everyone" (1 Corinthians 12:7 NOG). Different gifts, yes, but the Spirit is given to all believers, so that all can walk in the Spirit.

Surrendering to the Spirit

Walking in the Spirit is not overcoming something beyond you, but something beyond you overcoming you.

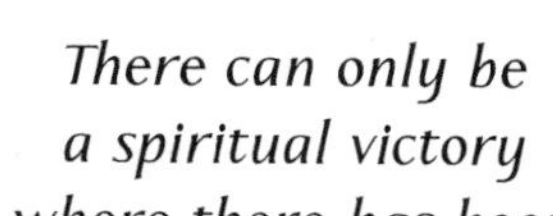

There can only be a spiritual victory where there has been a natural defeat.

Surrendering yourself to God never requires a lesson, but it requires a decision. All your studying is simply the diversion to delay what must be done.

There can only be a spiritual victory where there has been a natural defeat. God's Word says, "He who has died has been freed from sin" (Romans 6:7).

Walking in the Spirit is better stated as the Spirit walking in you. The Lord said, "And I will put my Spirit within you, and cause you to walk in my statutes, and ye shall keep my judgments, and do them" (Ezekiel 36:27 KJV).

The reason so few walk in the power of the Holy Spirit is not the scarcity of all that God has, but the scarcity of those willing to live the life so that they can receive all He has to give them.

Growing in the Spirit

To grow in the Spirit, you must first be born in the Spirit. If you're born, never think you'll grow apart from food. You need the Word as your food. If you're not in the Word, the Word is not in you. If the Word is not in you, it cannot change you. I cannot tell you how many weak Christians I've counseled, and when I ask them, "Are you in the Word?" their answer is always no. You must get in the Word.

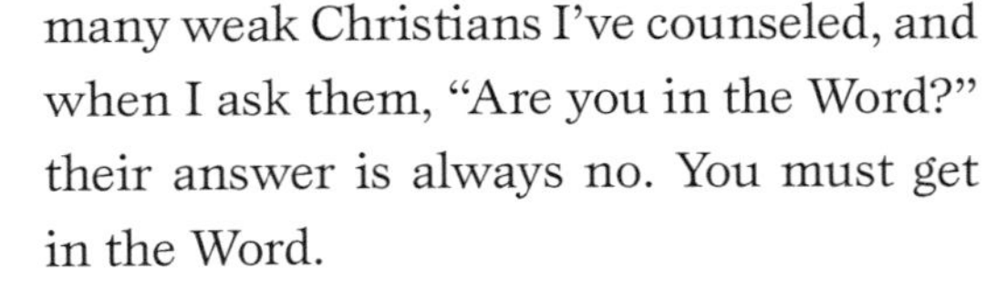

To grow spiritually, you must shrink naturally.

To grow spiritually, you must shrink naturally. The natural is the hindrance to the spiritual. This is why the minds that are highest in the natural will struggle the most to grow spiritually.

Do not just get knocked down by the Holy Spirit, but get back up and walk in the Spirit.

You do not grow spiritually by your natural efforts, but by the Holy Spirit. "Be renewed in the spirit of your mind" (Ephesians 4:23).

Spiritual change requires spiritual work. The Holy Spirit alone is qualified to do this work. Your only task is to let Him have His way in you.

From the Natural to the Spiritual

Going from the natural to the spiritual is one of the hardest things you'll ever do in your faith journey. The reason it's so hard is that it cannot be accomplished by your efforts. And that's where people get stuck—trying harder and harder, yet getting nowhere. The secret is this: You need the Holy Spirit to help you, for there's no other way.

I was the most stubborn of all with making this change. I'm naturally disciplined, so much so that I can hurt myself. The Lord had to plop me down onto that potter's wheel again and again, beating me into a new thing, until finally I gave up. With God, the more pliable you are, the easier it will be. We make it far too hard on ourselves.

Walking in the Spirit does not come naturally. Your spiritual growth is hindered by all your natural efforts. "But the natural [unbelieving] man does not accept the things [the teachings and revelations] of the Spirit of God, for they are foolishness [absurd and illogical] to him" (1 Corinthians 2:14 AMP).

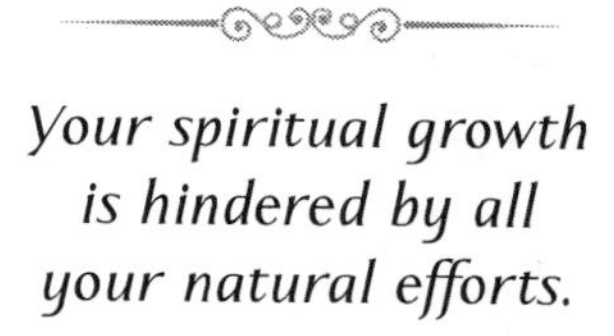

Your spiritual growth is hindered by all your natural efforts.

In the flesh, we gravitate toward that which satisfies the flesh. The same is true in the Spirit.

We desire to walk in the Spirit, yet we think we can do so by natural means. We are all just naturally proud. Humility is the antidote for pride.

I am convinced that the higher faith quickly loses the masses—not because they are too weak, but because they are too strong. We must be weak, so that it is His strength that rules within us. "That's why I take pleasure in my weaknesses, and in the insults, hardships, persecutions, and troubles that I suffer for Christ. For when I am weak, then I am strong" (2 Corinthians 12:10 NLT).

It is always in the reasoning of man that you will be limited in the power of God.

The Lord said, "I will give you a new heart and put a new spirit within you; I will take the heart of stone out of your flesh and give you a heart of flesh" (Ezekiel 36:26). Your stony heart is the stone tablet of the law. You couldn't keep the law. The heart of flesh is the Spirit of Christ in you. He can keep the law. This is how you can walk in the Spirit and not fulfill the lust of your flesh, by letting the Holy Spirit empower you with the life of Christ within you.

We're all growing in the Spirit. Just start from where you are, and know that the lessons will last a lifetime. We may trip, we may fall, but just keep getting back up. God knows you're weak. He doesn't expect you to be strong on your own, but to rely upon Him. Commit in your heart that you will do this. Someday you'll look back and see how far the Lord has moved you.

A Prayer for Walking in the Spirit

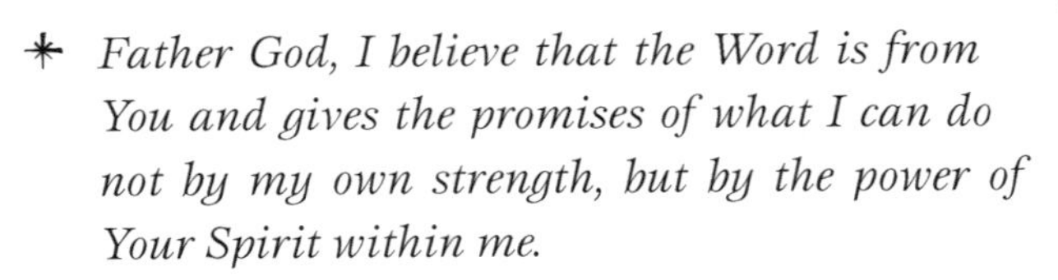

- *Father God, I believe that the Word is from You and gives the promises of what I can do not by my own strength, but by the power of Your Spirit within me.*

- *Lord Jesus, I know that just as You breathed the Holy Spirit upon Your disciples, You have the same Holy Spirit available to me in this day. Help me to realize the power of the Holy Spirit within me.*

- *Holy Spirit, pour into me with a greater measure, that I would be emptied of all self and filled with You. Help me to walk in the Spirit.*

Spiritual Guide

* If you aren't already serving God in some way, start doing so. He doesn't call those who are able, but He will enable those who answer His call. Whether it be ministering to your children, a class, or a nation, let the Holy Spirit lead you today. "For you, brethren, have been called to liberty; only do not use liberty as an opportunity for the flesh, but through love serve one another" (Galatians 5:13).

* If you hear something that you think is from the Holy Spirit, always test yourself by the Word of God. "Be diligent to present yourself approved to God, a worker who does not need to be ashamed, rightly dividing the word of truth" (2 Timothy 2:15).

* Get a mentor who's strong in faith. You're never too old for a mentor and never too young to be taught. I find that it's the prideful ones who reject mentoring and then fall into many errors. "Likewise you younger people, submit yourselves to your elders. Yes, all of you be submissive to one another, and be clothed with humility, for 'God resists the proud, but gives grace to the humble'" (1 Peter 5:5).

15 Hearing the Holy Spirit

The first step to hearing the Holy Spirit is believing that you can. He can speak, but will you listen?

"Therefore, as the Holy Spirit says: 'Today, if you will hear His voice...'" (Hebrews 3:7).

One Sunday several years ago my wife Mary and I went out to dinner after I had spent the day doing ministry in prison. I had the privilege to bring the Word for two services that day. I was quite hungry since I hadn't eaten since the day before. I always fast when I do ministry. I've found that when we deny the flesh, the Spirit has more room from which to work.

The waiter came to take our order. He was a worldly looking young man, with that new unkempt hairstyle and a few things

Too often, the mask we wear is the man or woman we are not.

pierced here or there. We shouldn't judge a book by its cover; often the cover hides the truth. Too often, the mask we wear is the man or woman we are not. I knew some of the toughest looking men and women in prison who had a bigger heart for God than many believers I know outside prison. I've also known some of the best-dressed people on the outside who have such cruelty deep within their hearts. We need to let the Lord show us the hearts of men and women. "For the LORD does not see as man sees; for man looks at the outward appearance, but the LORD looks at the heart" (1 Samuel 16:7).

After this young man took our order, I got a word from the Holy Spirit for him: "Tell him to step into the ministry and become a pastor." I often get words for people while doing ministry, but this was only the second time I got a word to give to a stranger out in public. I felt the "burden of the Lord." A burden of the Lord is like a weight or a twisting of the arm, such that you must do it, so the burden can then be lifted.

In the prophetic books of the Bible, we often see how the prophets were moved to give a word. Malachi said he had "the burden of the word of the LORD" (Malachi 1:1), and then he spoke the burden. I think many of us get this leading from the Lord in many areas of our lives. Believe that the Lord can move us all, not just the prophets of old. When you get the burden, you will know, because He won't let go of you until you've spoken what He has given you to say.

When this young waiter came back to the table, I prefaced the word for him with this: "God loves you very much and wants you to know something." Before I could give the word, he said to me, "Oh, I know God loves me. I'm in seminary, and I'm going to become a pastor."

Never doubt that God can use you. You have no idea the simple word the Lord may give you for someone else, and what it might mean to them. Often it's just an encouragement. I once got a word to tell a young wayward man in prison that God loves him. The next week, I saw that young man give his life to the Lord. Never doubt that the Holy Spirit can lead you in ministry. "Then the Spirit said to Philip, 'Go near and overtake this chariot'" (Acts 8:29)—and the man in that chariot was then saved for all eternity.

Never doubt that God can use you.

When we serve others, the Lord is teaching us while we serve them. The word for the waiter was a confirmation that helped me to be bolder in ministering to others. It helped me to know that I was discerning the voice of the Holy Spirit. It was a crazy word I got, but a good word. It also showed me that ministry is wherever I am. I learned the lesson of not adding my own words. Had I just spoken the word as it was given, it would have encouraged this young man so much more. We add too much of our own words. Oh, how much we need to stay teachable that we might learn!

I want you to know that the Holy Spirit speaks. If you're a believer, then believe. There's no program to learn how to hear Him. It will come by your drawing ever nearer to the Lord. Start every day in prayer and devotion and waiting on the Lord. Sometimes pray with your mouth closed and your ears open.

If you're a believer, then believe.

I just read the Word and believe. The Word says, "It shall come about after this that I shall pour out My Spirit on all mankind; and your sons and your daughters will prophesy, your old men will dream dreams, your young men will see visions" (Joel 2:28 AMP).

The pouring out of His Spirit has happened, if we will only receive it.

I want you to know that if God can speak through a donkey, He can speak through you. "Then the LORD opened the mouth of the donkey, and she said..." (Numbers 22:28).

You may go to a church where they don't teach that the Holy Spirit speaks. If so, take it to the Lord, seek the Holy Spirit, and pray that you will hear a word. Don't criticize or reject your church; love the church, and pray for your church. We have enough people against the church; we need more who are for it. Don't criticize your pastor; pray for your pastor. If you criticize your church or pastor, consider that you may be standing arm-in-arm with the devil.

Whatever church I go to, I always find that there's a remnant in the church of those few precious believers who are walking in the Spirit. Find the remnant. *If you can't find the remnant, be the remnant.* Respect those churches that are protecting their flock from wrong spirits, and pray for them that they might welcome the movement of the Holy Spirit.

If you can't find the remnant, be the remnant.

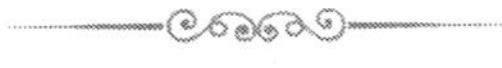

You don't have to be a prophet to prophesy. Be thankful for that. A prophet holds an office with much suffering and little comfort. If you wonder if you're called to be a prophet, are you ready to lose your head, to be killed by stoning, or to be sawn in two? No real prophet wants the office. Be satisfied to be a man or woman of God, because that is enough.

We are but utensils in the hands of God, yet we argue about whether we are a spoon or a fork.

You can find a hundred schools for prophets, but you never see a school for evangelists. Stop chasing the office of the prophet, and just do what the Lord has called you to do.

We are but utensils in the hands of God, yet we argue about whether we are a spoon or a fork.

Just serve Him and let people call you what they will. It is what He calls you that matters anyway.

Never seek the title—let the title seek you.

Giving a word to others in public is not something I flow in a lot. And I haven't always been obedient, including with this waiter that one night many years ago. There was one evening sometime before this incident where I had a word from the Lord for a waitress. I resisted, since I wasn't confident in the word I received for her. This was my first time in getting a word in public for a complete stranger. The Lord had simply told me to tell her that He loved her so much.

I continued to resist and didn't act on this word. He continued to press upon me until I thought I would collapse if I didn't obey Him. Finally, I got up and went looking for her, but she was nowhere to be found. She had gone, and I never saw her again. Later that night I got a word from the Lord that she had desperately needed that word. My disobedience was costly. I determined to never resist Him in this way again. Child of God, when the Lord presses hard on you, yield to Him.

We need to learn from our mistakes and know that the Lord gives us grace in them. Even in our mistakes, He is using us to His glory. Never let your shortcomings be a regret; instead, let each one be a learning experience which the Lord is using to teach you. Nobody in ministry is perfect. We're all learning. Don't let your pride get in the way of the Lord teaching you where you're wrong. And don't be afraid to admit your mistakes to others, since by sharing our shortcomings we bless others as they struggle in their own.

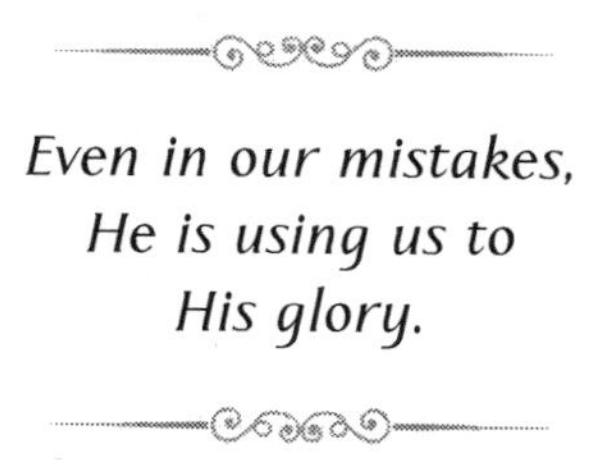
Even in our mistakes,
He is using us to
His glory.

I don't share my mistakes to present myself as humble, since I fail in that too. Rather, I want to encourage others who are learning to hear the Holy Spirit with greater clarity. I want to help them to not be set back by their failures. I can tell you a hundred stories where the Lord gave me words for people, and I was obedient, and we were all blessed.

The Lord teaches us more in our failures than in our successes. It's in the failures that He is preparing His servants for the greater works He has in mind for them to do. Learn to fail with grace.

A Prayer for Hearing the Holy Spirit

- *Father God, help me to not be so consumed in myself and in what I'm doing during the day that I miss that man or woman You place in front of me so that I might minister to them.*
- *Lord Jesus, show me how to be humble and not self-seeking in ministry, and to be serving You in whatever small or mundane things You might have me do.*
- *Holy Spirit, give me confirmations so that I know I'm discerning Your voice, and can act upon Your words with confidence.*

Spiritual Guide

- Give yourself grace in your mistakes as you're ministering, knowing that God does. "And God is able to make all grace abound toward you, that you, always having all sufficiency in all things, may have an abundance for every good work" (2 Corinthians 9:8).

* It's better to serve lower and rightly than higher and wrongly. Learn to discern His voice before you dare give a word to another, lest you be a mouthpiece of the devil. "The prophets prophesy falsely, and the priests rule by their own power; and My people love to have it so. But what will you do in the end?" (Jeremiah 5:31).

* When you do discern His voice, be faithful to act upon it. "The prophet who has a dream, let him tell a dream; and he who has My word, let him speak My word faithfully" (Jeremiah 23:28).

16 Praying in the Spirit

Natural prayers move men. Praying in the Spirit moves God.

"But you, beloved, building yourselves up on your most holy faith, praying in the Holy Spirit, keep yourselves in the love of God, looking for the mercy of our Lord Jesus Christ unto eternal life" (Jude 20–21).

Several years ago, my wife Mary and I took her father to our church. He was very ill, and the church elders had asked us to bring him there for prayer. I was young in my faith, and up until that time had only an introductory and textbook understanding of the things of God.

I expected the same type of group prayers that I'd seen and heard before. This was a very conservative church, so I expected a conservative prayer. (This is not a critique on the conservative church, for it's the conservative church that keeps the faith grounded. We need all the body.)

The prayer meeting quickly became different from anything I'd seen before. I've learned that church leaders are sometimes more conservative in the pulpit than they are in the prayer rooms. The elders laid hands on my wife's father, then went into a deep spiritual prayer like I'd never seen or heard before. They were speaking and murmuring all at once with such beautiful sounds. It was a chorus of holiness. I couldn't understand as much as I could sense.

Then something happened that I was completely unprepared for. There was something moving through the room like a wind, but not a wind. I felt it as if this wind was going right through me. It wasn't some hair-tingling feeling caused by emotions, but something that moved right through me. I didn't know what to make of it.

Afterward, I didn't speak a word to Mary about what happened. I knew it was something wonderful, but I simply had nothing I could reference to explain it. Was it just me?

Finally, a few days later, I asked Mary, and she told me she had felt it in the same way I had. God brings us the confirmation we need so that we grow in our understanding of Him.

Child of God, I want you to know that there's a level of prayer beyond the natural that reaches into heaven. We can pray in the Spirit such that we touch the things of God. The Holy Spirit is here with us right now, and the Spirit in us can elevate our prayers right into the throne room of heaven.

Praying in the Spirit is learned not in the classroom, but in the prayer closet.

To pray in the Spirit, the Spirit must first be in you.

Never wonder why you remain in the world that you hold onto so tightly. To pray

Praying in the Spirit is learned not in the classroom, but in the prayer closet.

in the Spirit, you have to let go of the natural. "A person who isn't spiritual doesn't accept the teachings of God's Spirit. He thinks they're nonsense. He can't understand them because a person must be spiritual to evaluate them" (1 Corinthians 2:14 NOG).

We have a Holy Spirit who cannot be contained within the textbooks of man.

We have a Holy Spirit who cannot be contained within the textbooks of man.

Naturally strong men can pray only weak prayers. It's the broken man who can pray in the Spirit, because he must rely upon the Spirit.

You can experience the Holy Spirit in your life. You can pray in the Spirit, and once you do, your prayer life will never be the same again. We need to be weak before God so that God will be strong in us. When you pray, learn to surrender yourself to the Holy Spirit who dwells within you, so that He will manifest the life of Christ within you, and your life becomes a prayer.

If you want to preach in the Spirit, you must first pray in the Spirit. Let this be you: "Pray at all times, with all kinds of prayers and requests, in the Spirit, vigilantly and persistently, for all God's people. And pray for me, too, that whenever I open my mouth, the words will be given to me to be bold in making known the secret of the Good News" (Ephesians 6:18-19 CJB).

If you want to preach in the Spirit, you must first pray in the Spirit.

Learn to pray for others more than you pray for yourself. As the Spirit moves in you, there will be a prayer that goes through you. Let the Spirit lead you on what you might pray for. There is a principle where intercessory prayer is more powerful because it is selfless, and in that selflessness it fulfills all the law of God. "For all the law is fulfilled in one word, even in this: 'You shall love your neighbor as yourself'" (Galatians 5:14).

Natural prayers ask for only natural things. "For those who live according to the flesh set their minds on the things of the flesh, but those who live according to the Spirit, the things of the Spirit" (Romans 8:5).

Natural prayers seek His approval of your will. Spiritual prayers seek His will, so that you would be approved.

"And when they had prayed, the place where they were assembled together was shaken; and they were all filled with the Holy Spirit, and they spoke the word of God with boldness" (Acts 4:31). *You know you are praying in the Spirit when even the building can't sit still.*

Whatever fills you defines you. If you are not filled with the Holy Spirit, you are full of just yourself. Beware the intellectually filled man who is empty of the Spirit of God.

When we pray in the Spirit, it's not only so that God will hear us, but so that we would hear Him. God is Spirit, and it's by the Holy Spirit that we hear Him. We need to pray higher that we can reach heaven. Prayer is not only to ask for things from God, but for God to ask for things from you.

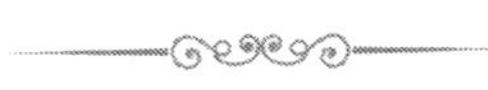

Prayer is not only to ask for things from God, but for God to ask for things from you.

Prayers without words speak the loudest. "In the same way the Spirit also helps our weakness; for we do not know how to pray as we should, but the Spirit Himself intercedes for us with groanings too deep for words" (Romans 8:26 NASB).

In your prayers, don't try to lower the Lord into your plans, but ask Him to raise you into His.

You know you are praying in the Spirit when you can hear the Spirit. "As they ministered to the Lord and fasted, the Holy Spirit said, 'Now separate to Me Barnabas and Saul for the work to which I have called them.'" (Acts 13:2-3).

Praying in the Spirit is not an intellectual principle that you can learn with your natural mind. Rather, it's a spiritual truth that must be given to you. The great divide between those who progress spiritually and those who don't is this: To increase spiritually, you must decrease naturally. The more you have to lose in the natural, the harder it is to let go of it. The hardest thing for a person to do is to simply give up.

The Holy Spirit will move in you only when you let Him. Otherwise, try as you might, you're only getting in His way. If you want to become proficient in praying in the Spirit, it will be by becoming absolutely surrendered to God in your life.

Fasting separates you from the natural so that you can step into the spiritual.

Natural prayers can touch the heart of man, but praying in the Spirit places you in the heart of God. "Build yourselves up on the foundation of your most holy faith by praying every moment in the Spirit. Fasten your hearts to the love of God" (Jude 20-21 TPT).

Natural prayers can touch the heart of man, but praying in the Spirit places you in the heart of God.

Ask the Holy Spirit to teach you to pray in the Holy Spirit. The Lord Jesus taught, "The Holy Spirit, whom the Father will send in My name, will teach you everything" (John 14:26 NOG).

Your spiritual growth and your prayer life go together. You won't grow spiritually if your prayer life is lacking. And your prayer life will be lacking if you have no spiritual growth. If you want to

Your spiritual growth and your prayer life go together.

grow spiritually, then pray for that. Often the reason we don't get things is that we don't ask for them.

As you pray more often, you'll find you pray with less effort. Prayer is not a chore but a privilege. Until we see prayer as a blessing, we don't understand prayer at all. Prayer is not only asking but declaring, settling in your mind how great and loving our heavenly Father truly is.

When we pray in the Spirit, we're reaching into the Spirit of God. It's in the Spirit of God where we find the heart of the Father. When we pray in the Father's heart and in His desires, we'll be praying in the will of God. When we pray in His will, our prayers are heard by Him. "Now this is the confidence that we have in Him, that if we ask anything according to His will, He hears us" (1 John 5:14).

Wherever you lack understanding on the things of God, pray in the Spirit about them. It will be by the Spirit that you'll gain in yourself the Spirit of wisdom and revelation. This wisdom and revelation are not from the things of man, but from the things of heaven.

We see in the Word that the Lord Jesus often went off and prayed alone. There's something special in private prayer, where pretense and pride have no place to take hold, and the believer lies prostrate before a mighty God. See to it that you don't neglect your private time with the Father, so that by His Holy Spirit you reach to the throne room of heaven to spend time with Him. Make it your mission to spend more and more time in prayer, and your spiritual life will grow and flourish for the kingdom.

A Prayer for Praying in the Holy Spirit

* Father God, I want to feel Your heart beating. I want to pray to You in the Spirit so that I can reach Your Spirit and pray in Your will over my life and the lives of those around me.

* Lord Jesus, help me to be willing to go off by myself as You did to pray all through the night. Help me to have such a life of prayer that my life *is* prayer.

* Holy Spirit, help me to pray in the will of the Father. Pray through me, Holy Spirit, with those deep things that cannot even be spoken aloud. I want Your prayers to be through me for those around me.

Spiritual Guide

* Choose a special place in your home where you'll pray deeper prayers. Make this a place where you pray deep into the spiritual realm. "But you, when you pray, go into your room, and when you have shut your door, pray to your Father who is in the secret place; and your Father who sees in secret will reward you openly" (Matthew 6:6).

* Be prepared to battle as you pray in the Spirit. There's nothing to fear in prayer, but there's much that will come against you. Stand firm and know that God is with you. "For we are not fighting against flesh-and-blood enemies, but against evil rulers and authorities of the unseen world, against mighty powers in

this dark world, and against evil spirits in the heavenly places" (Ephesians 6:12).

- Keep pressing in to pray more often and more fervently, that your prayers would move mountains. When you pray in the Spirit, you're tapping into the unlimited resources of heaven. "The effective, fervent prayer of a righteous man avails much" (James 5:16).

17 Prophetic Dreams

You can be inspired by the words of men, but a word from the Lord changes the course of your life.

"For God may speak in one way, or in another, yet man does not perceive it. In a dream, in a vision of the night, when deep sleep falls upon men, while slumbering on their beds, then He opens the ears of men, and seals their instruction" (Job 33:14–16).

How much we need to encourage people to listen and then obey the voice of the Lord. When the Lord speaks, there's always a reason. We must learn to listen, and we must then learn to obey. I've been most blessed to hear from the Lord in many different ways and about so many different things. I'm careful to make sure that it's His voice and not my own, nor deceptive words from the evil one. But when I know that it's His voice, I'm confident in all He tells me.

When the Lord speaks, there's always a reason.

When I was a young man, I met the sweetest and most gentle young lady I've ever known, and her name was Mary. We quickly fell in love, and within months we were married. We've been married for over thirty-five years at the time of this writing. In all that time, she has never raised her voice to me, nor have I raised mine to her. There are some blessings that can be attributed only to the Lord. "He who finds a wife finds a good thing, and obtains favor from the LORD" (Proverbs 18:22).

A few years ago, I wrote a short article about when the Lord came to me in a dream and gave me a prophetic word that saved Mary's life. He did this just a few days before our wedding anniversary. I don't know why the Lord chooses to act when He does, but I trust that He always can.

Here's what I wrote about that day:

Never doubt that the Lord can give you a word.

Never doubt that the Lord can give you a word. He has spoken to men and women throughout history. To this very day, He hasn't stopped talking to us. Oh, the great benefits to that blessed believer who would be obedient to the word of the Lord! "Your own ears will hear Him. Right behind you a voice will say, 'This is the way you should go," whether to the right or to the left'" (Isaiah 30:21 NLT).

It's never a question of whether the Lord will speak to you—but of whether you will listen.

It's never a question of whether the Lord will speak to you—but of whether you will listen. Jesus said, "My sheep hear My voice, and I know them, and they follow Me" (John 10:27).

The goal of drawing near to God is not so He will hear you better, but so that you will hear Him better. He already knows what you will say, but you need to get a word from Him.

Never limit the way in which the Lord might speak to you.

Seek to live a holy life such that His holy words would be in the path in which you are walking.

Always be deep in the Word of God so you can be sure that the voice you're hearing is His. "And the sheep follow him, for they know his voice" (John 10:4).

Sometimes the Lord will give you a strong word, and sometimes a gentle whisper. Sometimes He'll give you a word for yourself; at other times He gives you a word for someone else. Sometimes He comes in your thoughts; at other times He comes in a dream or a vision. "I will pour out My Spirit on all flesh…your old men shall dream dreams, your young men shall see visions" (Joel 2:28).

If you want Him to come to you, then you must draw near to Him yourself. Live in His presence, and His presence will be ever near to you. "Draw near to God and He will draw near to you" (James 4:8).

On March 13, 2017, my wife Mary wasn't feeling well at all. She had symptoms of a prior condition and had called her doctor to get the same medicine that had resolved it before. I was just about to lie down to rest for a while, and I told her to immediately wake me if she needed me.

Right before I lay down, I read something I'd heard from the Holy Spirit and had written down just a few days prior: "*You can be inspired by the words of men, but a word from the Lord changes the course of your life.*"

"You can be inspired by the words of men, but a word from the Lord changes the course of your life."

As soon as I lay down, I fell asleep. In a dream, I heard this from the Lord about Mary: "Her appendix needs to come out." I don't often hear from the Lord in my dreams, but I know His voice. I woke up with those words still in my thoughts. Friends, the Lord still speaks to this very day.

Child of God, do you believe the Word of God? Jesus said, "When the Spirit of Truth comes, He will guide you into all the truth; for He will not speak on his own initiative but will say only what He hears. He will also announce to you the events of the future" (John 16:13 CJB).

While I was still lying in bed, Mary texted me, and I went to see her. She wasn't feeling well, her complexion looked really bad, and she was shaking. I'd never seen her look so ill before. I held her close and prayed over her. I told her we needed to take her to the hospital. But she said the doctors would call back soon and prescribe the medicine she needed.

I didn't want to alarm her with the word the Lord had given me. I told her that perhaps she had a different problem from the one she had before, even though the symptoms were the same. But she insisted it was the same problem as before. I wasn't going to yield. I remember telling her, "Either you can get dressed and I'll take you to the hospital, or I'll call 911 and they'll take you just as you are." She got up and got dressed. I took my precious wife to the hospital.

When we were in the emergency room, a nurse was taking our information. She asked us, "Is there any faith reason that would affect how we would care for you." I told her, "Yes, if our God chooses to do a miracle, then we won't be needing any help from you." It was so precious as we then found out this nurse was a believer, and we had a wonderful conversation with her about how God had worked in her life. She'd been orphaned into the foster care system as a child, but a family took her in and raised her in the faith. There are so many rich stories of the grace of God all around us.

The doctors took Mary away and proceeded to do some tests to see what was going on. When she came back to the emergency room where I was waiting, the doctor came in and told us my wife would have to be admitted for surgery right away. I already knew what the surgery would be for. The doctor confirmed what the Lord had already revealed to me earlier, that she would have to have her appendix taken out.

Before her surgery, I told Mary about how the Lord had given me the word of what was wrong with her. I anointed her with oil and prayed that the Lord would protect her. I prayed for the Lord to be with her and with the doctors and nurses. "Is anyone among you sick? Let him call for the elders of the church, and let them pray over him, anointing him with oil in the name of the Lord. And the prayer of faith will save the sick" (James 5:14-15). Friends, we need more prayers of faith.

After her surgery, the surgeon came out to speak with me. He said that her appendix had burst and had become infectious. But somehow, the infection hadn't spread, but was contained in an area where he was able to remove it all. Somehow indeed! I'm convinced that the many prayer warriors who were praying for Mary held back the infection by the power of God through their prayers. "Pray for one another, that you may be healed. The effective, fervent prayer of a righteous man avails much" (James 5:16).

Never doubt that the Lord can speak to you, even in a dream. "I will pour out My Spirit on all flesh...your old men shall dream dreams" (Joel 2:28).

Nothing is impossible in your dreams, and that is why God will sometimes meet you there.

Nothing is impossible in your dreams, and that is why God will sometimes meet you there.

When I posted this article on my Facebook ministry page, one man become very angry at me. He was critical of what I posted and said that God no longer speaks to us in this day. I thanked him for his views. I've learned that it doesn't help to argue with people who are bent on believing that the power of God has somehow been diminished in our day. I remember telling Mary afterward that it was a good thing God didn't have her married to that man.

A Prayer for the Lord to Meet Us in Our Dreams

- *Father God, help me to walk in Your ways so that You can use me to be a blessing to my friends and family around me. Help me to believe that You're still at work in the lives of those who follow You.*

- *Lord Jesus, pray for me that I will have the right motives in seeking a deeper filling of the Holy Spirit. Help me to serve You in humility, so that I could be useful for the kingdom.*

- *Holy Spirit, pour into me wisdom and revelation, that I would have Your fullness working through me. Help me to hear You, so that I can help those around me.*

Spiritual Guide

- When we pray, we ask for what we want. Make notes in your daily journal of what you pray for, of the things that weigh most on your heart. Prayers reveal God to us, and then the Holy Spirit can reveal our hearts to God. "Likewise the Spirit also helps in our weaknesses. For we do not know what we should pray for as we ought, but the Spirit Himself makes intercession for us with groanings which cannot be uttered" (Romans 8:26).

- If you aren't already reading God's Word every day, commit to doing this. His Word is the bread of life, our spiritual life. Our spirit would starve if we didn't consume God's Word every day.

"Desire the pure milk of the word, that you may grow thereby" (1 Peter 2:2).

* Pick one verse each week to hold onto and memorize. If you can't memorize it, write it down where you can read it every day. The Word can change you if you let it. "Your word I have hidden in my heart, that I might not sin against You" (Psalm 119:11).

18

Desiring Spiritual Gifts

Your greatest barrier to the higher calling is your wrong desire for it.

"You are so passionate about embracing the manifestations of the Holy Spirit! Now become even more passionate about the things that strengthen the entire church" (1 Corinthians 14:12 TPT).

Desiring spiritual gifts is good, since God can use them through you to help others. But believers must first be prepared so that their gifts won't cause them to become prideful. Whenever we think anything of ourselves as we operate in a spiritual gift, we're being a hindrance to what God is trying to do through us. There's a great danger in the gifts, since they can cause our pride to swell. The greater our pride, the farther we'll be from God. This is why so few operate in spiritual gifts; God is protecting them from what the gifts would do to them.

Whenever I teach on surrendering or humility, I see little interest in those teachings. But when I teach on walking in the power of the Holy Spirit, people will be much more interested. But the truth is, these teachings must go together, for you won't operate in the fullness of the Holy Spirit without also being surrendered in humility before God. That's why so few reach very high in their spiritual potential. They squander what God might do through them, because their focus is on how men might see them instead of how God might use them.

I've often seen people chase spiritual gifts so that they could be elevated above those around them. Some people see spiritual gifts like they do their cars or their clothes—as just another way to impress others. They try to use spiritual power to gain a natural position. So long as you seek a gift to be elevated, you're wrong. Pride stands in opposition to the kingdom of God. It's better to have no gifts than to use gifts wrongly.

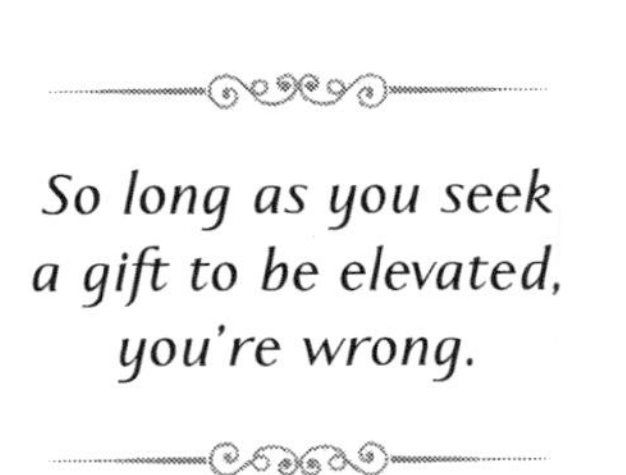
So long as you seek a gift to be elevated, you're wrong.

Get in prayer before you ever seek to have God pour a spiritual gift into you. Bow down low to the ground, and be willing to serve in obscurity, so that God will get all the glory in how He used you. Child of God, get yourself right before God, and then you'll be ready to serve others. You were meant to receive a spiritual gift, so prepare yourself that He might now give it to you. Surrender yourself. Walk in humility. Be ready for any gift He might give you.

We need the presence of the Holy Spirit before we flow in the power of the Holy Spirit.

If the Holy Spirit reigns in you, it will show. "But the Holy Spirit produces this kind of fruit in our lives: love, joy, peace, patience, kindness, goodness, faithfulness, gentleness, and self-control" (Galatians 5:22-23 NLT).

If the Holy Spirit reigns in you, it will show.

God will rarely give you a spiritual gift you aren't ready for. Give your life to Him, and let Him give you what you need, when you need it, and when you're ready for it.

After the apostle Paul taught on spiritual gifts in 1 Corinthians 12, he wrote the next chapter teaching on the greatest gift, which is love. Love is the first and foremost fruit that comes from the Holy Spirit. Spiritual gifts and love are inseparable. You cannot take hold of a gift from the Holy Spirit and let go of love. As Paul taught us, "Earnestly desire the best gifts. And yet I show you a more excellent way" (1 Corinthians 12:31).

Seek the fruit of the Spirit first, and let the spiritual gifts come after. "Pursue love! However, keep on eagerly seeking the things of the Spirit" (1 Corinthians 14:1 CJB).

Desire the gifts but hold onto the better way of love while you are waiting. Paul taught, "And though I have the gift of prophecy, and understand all mysteries and all knowledge, and though I have all faith, so that I could remove mountains, but have not love, I am nothing" (1 Corinthians 13:2).

Seek the fruit of the Spirit first, and let the spiritual gifts come after.

We're only the violin in the hands of God, and the music that comes is only by His power and to His glory. Once the song is over, the violin must then be set down. Until you learn to be nothing for Him, He cannot be everything through you. Unless you're willing to serve in humility, your flesh still reigns in your ministry.

Spiritual gifts are not for you, but to be through you.

What we desire, has us.

Stop seeking the gifts of the Spirit while thinking you might then start serving God with them. Instead serve God as you are, and He'll provide the gifts you need in the midst of your serving. "Now there are different kinds of gifts, but the same Spirit gives them… to each person is given the particular manifestation of the Spirit that will be for the common good" (1 Corinthians 12:4,7 CJB).

When we're happily married, all we want is to be with our spouse. We're with them not to gain gifts, since we see them as our greatest gift. That's how we're to be with our heavenly Father. If we ever seek the gift over the Giver, we're in error.

Spiritual gifts are not for you, but to be through you.

The reason many don't operate in spiritual gifts is that they want to be seen more than to serve.

Spiritual gifts are not to turn men's eyes toward you, but to turn their eyes toward God. Our gifts aren't meant to replace God in our life, but to reflect God in our life. "Each of you as a good manager must use the gift that God has given you to serve others" (1 Peter 4:10 NOG).

I would rather walk in a lower gifting that's right than to have a higher gifting with errors. Nobody stumbles on their knees.

Spiritual gifts are for producing heavenly outcomes. Whenever we try to use them for our self-promotion, we violate the foundation of holiness from which they came. It would be better to not have a gift than to corrupt the gift by handling it wrongly. We will be judged for how well we steward each gift we're given.

Spiritual gifts are not to turn men's eyes toward you, but to turn their eyes toward God.

Never let the things you do for God become more important to you than God. "You shall love the LORD your God with all your heart, with all your soul, and with all your strength" (Deuteronomy 6:5).

Never let the things you do for God become more important to you than God.

The Holy Spirit is not for sale, and He is not for your promotion. "And when Simon saw that through the laying on of the apostles' hands the Holy Spirit was given, he offered them money, saying, 'Give me this power also, that anyone on whom I lay hands may receive the Holy Spirit.' But Peter said to him, 'Your money perish with you, because you thought that the gift of God could be purchased with money!'" (Acts 8:18-20).

If you want to serve God rightly with spiritual gifts, it will always promote Him and demote you. See to it that you either get this right, or sit down.

A Prayer to Rightly Desire Spiritual Gifts

✶ *Father God, help me to desire spiritual gifts only in order to serve You. Help me to give You all the glory for anything You might do through me.*

✶ *Lord Jesus, help me to remain humble before You, willing to have nothing in me that would build up my pride and separate myself from You.*

✶ *Holy Spirit, help me to seek gifts only to serve the Father, and give me the desire to choose humility before serving, that my serving would be holy.*

Spiritual Guide

- When you pray, make declarations verbally. A word spoken has more power than a thought concealed. "With my voice I cry out to the LORD; with my voice I plead for mercy to the LORD" (Psalm 142:1 ESV).

- Write out one verse every day. Then write out what that verse means to you, and what God is trying to tell you. Then apply into your life what He's telling you. His Word is living, but it lives in you only if you let it. "For we have the living Word of God, which is full of energy, and it pierces more sharply than a two-edged sword.... It interprets and reveals the true thoughts and secret motives of our hearts" (Hebrews 4:12 TPT).

- In your prayer journal, write out declarations of deliverance from whatever darkness holds you. For example, write out, "I rebuke in the name of Jesus this pattern of anger within me, where I'm lashing out at those around me." To walk in the Spirit, you must learn to consecrate yourself from the ways of this world. "And do not be conformed to this world, but be transformed by the renewing of your mind, that you may prove what is that good and acceptable and perfect will of God" (Romans 12:2).

19

Activating Spiritual Gifts

The hindrance to walking in your own spiritual gift is your trying to walk in another's.

"God has given each of you a gift from his great variety of spiritual gifts. Use them well to serve one another" (1 Peter 4:10 NLT).

The nine gifts of the Holy Spirit are different gifts distributed to us as He sees fit, that we would then be useful for the kingdom. The Lord will choose our gift, and He will often choose the man or woman who will then activate that gift in us.

The Word of God tells us: "There are diversities of gifts, but the same Spirit. There are differences of ministries, but the same Lord. And there are diversities of activities, but it is the same God who works all in all. But the manifestation of the Spirit is given to each one for the profit of all:

[1] for to one is given the word of wisdom through the Spirit,

[2] to another the word of knowledge through the same Spirit,

[3] to another faith by the same Spirit,

[4] to another gifts of healings by the same Spirit,

[5] to another the working of miracles,

[6] to another prophecy,

[7] to another discerning of spirits,

[8] to another different kinds of tongues,

[9] to another the interpretation of tongues.

But one and the same Spirit works all these things, distributing to each one individually as He wills" (1 Corinthians 12:4-11).

We need a balanced teaching on spiritual gifts. On the one hand, we need believers to reach for and take hold of all that God would have for them. They must believe and know that God has poured out these gifts for His children to bless each other with, and that by the gifts of the Holy Spirit, we can do kingdom work like we could never do on our own. When we gain the gifts from heaven, we can accomplish more on earth than we could have ever dreamed possible in our own natural strength. It's the grandest privilege to be a vessel for the kingdom of God!

On the other hand, we must exercise great caution to not become hyper-focused on gifts so that we seek them for the wrong reasons, and in so doing cannot exercise these gifts with right motives. Avoiding this can be extremely hard, since there's often a great swelling of pride that comes after a believer first receives a gift. We must seek to serve God with humility and reverence as we exercise His gifts. If we don't, we risk losing the privilege of serving God with the powers from heaven.

Beloved child of God, be careful. Seek humility first, since with that foundation you'll be standing on holy ground when doing kingdom work. Pride has no place in the kingdom, and it must be cast out and kept out of a believer who's intent upon serving God rightly. Check yourself, examine yourself. To the degree you want to be seen by men, you're in error. Seek to be seen by God, and let men think of you what they will. Seek to serve God for His purposes, with His power, to His credit, to His glory, and from there you'll be a blessing to the kingdom.

I pray that you would prayerfully consider why you want the gifts before you seek the gifts. We often think our motives are better than they really are. It's when you're satisfied only with Him that He'll give anything more.

Motives trump actions in the kingdom of God.

Once you get the motives right, the gifts are soon to follow.

Activating Spiritual Gifts

My prayer is that believers will discover and walk in the spiritual gifts God has for them. Paul prayed, "For I long to see you, that I may impart to you some spiritual gift, so that you may be established" (Romans 1:11).

I'm blessed by my dear friend Bonnie Calkins, who many years ago laid hands on me and activated a spiritual gift into my life. Bonnie is a gifted prophetic teacher on end-times and the Bride of Christ. Bonnie prophesied over me to activate, prepare, and encourage me for the calling I would walk in. The spiritual gift imparted to me has flowed like a river since that day.

If you're overflowing in the Holy Spirit, and then you lay hands on someone, there's a spiritual power flowing through you and onto them. God is the power, and you're only the conduit. Jesus taught, "Anyone who believes in me may come and drink! For the Scriptures declare, 'Rivers of living water will flow from his heart.' (When he said 'living water,' He was speaking of the Spirit, who would be given to everyone believing in Him)" (John 7:38-39 NLT).

Every time I meet with Bonnie, I'm reminded of all that was imparted to me and the fruit that has come from it. Bonnie always encourages me to this day to stay diligent in serving the Lord. "Therefore I remind you to stir up the gift of God which is in you through the laying on of my hands" (2 Timothy 1:6).

Once you have received a spiritual gift, you must then walk in it. "Do not neglect the gift that is in you, which was given to you by prophecy with the laying on of the hands of the eldership" (1 Timothy 4:14).

Once you have received a spiritual gift, you must then walk in it.

Receiving a Spiritual Gift

The Lord will never give you a spiritual gift you aren't ready to receive. He loves you too much to allow you to have a gift you aren't prepared to walk in. Thank Him for not giving you what would ruin you. Be content with having nothing, and from there He can start to do a work in you.

The barrier to the gifts is in our pride, and pride is at the root of every wrong motive. Even after we receive a gift, there must be a continual humbling before God so that our motives remain pure, and so that He has the right of way in our hearts.

The first step in receiving a spiritual gift is to be filled of the Holy Spirit. "And when Paul had laid hands on them, the Holy Spirit came upon them, and they spoke with tongues and prophesied" (Acts 19:6).

It's by the Holy Spirit that you will gain a spiritual gift, and it's by the Holy Spirit that you can then walk in it. "But one and the same Spirit works all these things, distributing to each one individually as He wills" (1 Corinthians 12:11).

It's by the Holy Spirit that you will gain a spiritual gift, and it's by the Holy Spirit that you can then walk in it.

The great hindrance for people in receiving the gifts is pride, because pride stands tall between man and God. Either they want a gift to be seen by men, or they refuse to receive the gift through someone they think beneath them. Natural pride always blocks spiritual breakthroughs.

Our greatest need is to grow in humility, apart from which you'll be a hindrance to what the Holy Spirit can do through you for the kingdom. What great regret we will have in heaven when we realize all that we forfeited for the kingdom because of the pride we held in our hearts.

Spiritual gifts cannot be chosen, bought, or taken hold of, but only humbly received. The gifts are not for you, but through you, so that God makes you His vessel.

You can never take hold in the natural of what can be received as a gift only in the spiritual.

Your natural strength cannot lift a feather in the spiritual realm. "But the natural man does not receive the things of the Spirit of God" (1 Corinthians 2:14).

Your natural strength cannot lift a feather in the spiritual realm.

Spiritual gifts are not for you, but to be through you. "Since you're eager to have spiritual gifts, try to excel in them so that you help the church grow" (1 Corinthians 14:12 NOG).

God Chooses Your Spiritual Gifts

We will get different gifts, but we share in the same Holy Spirit. "There are different kinds of spiritual gifts, but the same Spirit is the source of them all" (1 Corinthians 12:4 NLT).

Don't worry about which gift you receive. Rejoice in the spiritual gift He has picked out just for you. "Each one has his own gift from God" (1 Corinthians 7:7).

In God's economy, every gift has equal value in what it can achieve for the kingdom.

We are but the violin in the hands of the Master. "As each one has received some spiritual gift, he should use it to serve others" (1 Peter 4:10 CJB).

We are but the violin in the hands of the Master.

We can have all the various spiritual gifts pour through us from time to time as the Lord sees fit. These temporary gifts we may walk in are to meet a specific need at a specific point in time. For example, the Lord gave me the "word of knowledge" gift when I was preaching in prison ministry. The Holy Spirit would show me in advance exactly who would receive salvation at a service, so that I would keep pressing into the altar call until that person came up. God never got it wrong, and this bolstered my faith and my preaching. But when God called me out of the prison ministry and I stopped preaching, I no longer needed that gift for what He had me doing in the next season.

He gives the right gift at the right time. Let Him be in charge; you aren't qualified, and neither am I. Don't ever chase the gift, since it isn't yours to take but only to receive. The Lord will guide us into the gift in which we'll flow the strongest. Once you've received a gift, if you ever feel like your gift isn't flowing as much as it used to, it's because you aren't yielding.

A river flows only when the ground has given way.

A river flows only when the ground has given way.

Don't seek the gift; seek the Giver, and surrender your life to Him. It's there that you'll find your gift by which you can then serve Him. "For God's gifts and his call can never be withdrawn" (Romans 11:29 NLT).

We live in a day where the pride of man rules in many churches. There are two extreme teachings in our churches today—either that the gifts are no more, or that the gifts are everything. The power of God still remains today—of that you can be certain. Read the Word of God and pray for the Holy Spirit to reveal this truth to you. My prayer is that more of God's children will walk in the gifts God has for them, to the benefit of their church and of those around them. Persevere in your faith, and know that with God all things are possible.

If you go to a church that doesn't teach that the gifts are still flowing, then press into the Lord for your gifts anyway, since it may be through you that the Lord will minister to the church you're in. If you go to a church that's too hyper-focused on the gifts, then be a servant of love so they can see that love is greater than the gifts.

Be patient in waiting for your gift as you serve Him. I served in ministry many years before the gifts started flowing in me. It's in our waiting that the Lord prepares our hearts to have the right motives. When we see someone with a gift, we don't always know what they went through before they received the gift. We don't know what God had to form in them through adversity so that they would remain humble as they served Him.

It's in adversity that the gifts are formed, and it's in adversity that the believer is prepared to walk in them. Never think that walking in the gifts is easy, since the opposite is true. Just read your Bible or the history books of old, and they'll prove the truth of this principle. But never fear adversity; when it comes, be sure that it will produce something far greater than you had before. The apostle Paul suffered greatly, yet he said, "For I consider that the sufferings of this present time are not worthy to be compared with the glory which shall be revealed in us" (Romans 8:18).

It's in adversity that the gifts are formed, and it's in adversity that the believer is prepared to walk in them.

A Prayer for Activating Spiritual Gifts

* *Father God, I would rather have You than a gift. I would rather be right in a lower gifting than wrong in a higher gifting. Help me to seek to please You in everything I do.*

* *Lord Jesus, help me to be a lowly servant, meek in my actions, humble in my spirit. I want to be known by You more than to be known by men.*

* *Holy Spirit, pour into and through me only in proportion to my humility before the Father. Help me never to draw attention to myself, but to Christ my Savior.*

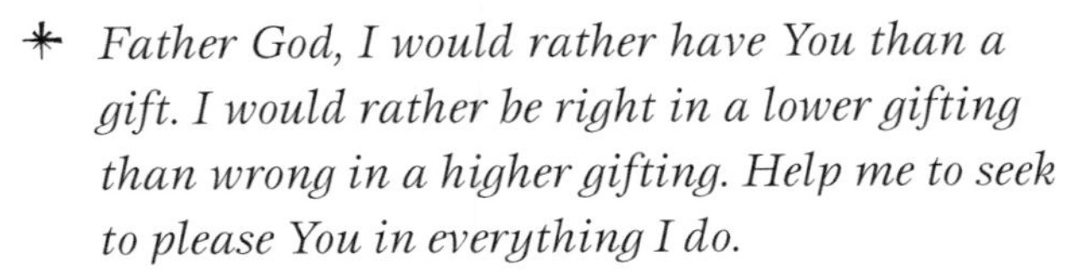

Spiritual Guide

* Don't be more zealous to gain a spiritual gift than you are to serve God with it. Get your motives right. "Even so you, since you are zealous for spiritual gifts, let it be for the edification of the church that you seek to excel" (1 Corinthians 14:12).

* Be satisfied with getting nothing more from Christ than Himself. "I have been crucified with Christ; it is no longer I who live, but Christ lives in me" (Galatians 2:20).

* Set your mind that you would rather be right in a lower gifting than wrong in a higher one. Be discerning on where you gain your teaching. "Beloved, do not believe every spirit, but test the spirits, whether they are of God; because many false prophets have gone out into the world" (1 John 4:1).

20 Yielding to the Holy Spirit

Growing spiritually has to do with yielding ground, not gaining ground. It is not gaining power, but relinquishing power, relinquishing your right to you.

"For those who live according to the flesh set their minds on the things of the flesh, but those who live according to the Spirit, the things of the Spirit. But you are not in the flesh but in the Spirit, if indeed the Spirit of God dwells in you" (Romans 8:5,9).

It's one thing to surrender yourself for a moment, and another to willingly yield yourself each day so that God can do a work in you. Rigid clay breaks, but yielded clay can be formed. In our ongoing yielding of ourselves the Father can shape us into what He has ordained for us to become.

The natural man always seeks what he might do by his own natural power. When we stand before spiritual mountains, they can never be ascended by natural strength. If we want to grow spiritually, we must learn to humble ourselves in the natural. The secret to growing spiritually is learning how to shrink in humility in the natural and then fall into the hands of God. The ones who grow most are not the strongest, but those who are yielding their life continually to God.

You cannot fill a cup until it is first empty.

The most powerful saints in the kingdom are those empty enough to be filled with God.

The greater the yielding to the Holy Spirit, the greater the filling of the Holy Spirit. "Never restrain or put out the fire of the Holy Spirit" (1 Thessalonians 5:19 TPT).

The measure that God is in your life is the measure of your life that you have yielded to God.

The greater the yielding to the Holy Spirit, the greater the filling of the Holy Spirit.

Any lack of growth is not a lack of power from God, but a lack of yielding from you. "God resists the proud" (James 4:6).

Your faith is not increased by striving, but by yielding. It is not what you do for God that matters as much as how much you let Him do in you.

Stop imagining spiritual growth will come in an instant or by your efforts. Spiritual growth isn't bound by natural time. The length of time of your journey isn't the only measure for how far you can go; your rate of progression must also be considered. The more yielded you are, the faster He can change you.

The greatest hindrance to spiritual growth is a stagnation in the life of the believer. Many say they want to grow, but only a few do what must be done so that growth can happen. It's your willingness to be nothing so that the Holy Spirit can be everything in you.

Growing spiritually is not something you do; it is your yielding to the Holy Spirit to do it in you.

You will not have the power of the Holy Spirit unless the power of the Holy Spirit first has you.

You don't take hold of the Holy Spirit—rather, the Holy Spirit takes hold of you. "And the Spirit of the LORD came mightily upon him" (Judges 14:6).

You won't be more if you do more. You will be more when you let Him do more in you.

You will not have the power of the Holy Spirit unless the power of the Holy Spirit first has you.

Spiritual growth never comes by natural methods, since your natural efforts only get in the way. The Lord does the work, and He will raise us up over time. Your growth has more to do with your prayer life and your time in the Word than your service. A plant never strives to grow, but only yields beneath the light and spreads its roots deep in the ground below. And so it is for Christians who want to grow spiritually; they must be in the light, spending time in prayer with the Lord, and spreading their roots deeply in the Word of God.

It is not what you give that reflects your heart, but what you refuse to let go of. The Lord Jesus said, "Sell all that you have and distribute to the poor, and you will have treasure in heaven; and come, follow Me" (Luke 18:22). *It is not the money the Lord wants; He is after your heart.*

Whatever you hold onto has a hold on you.

Whatever you refuse to give up is your god.

What you refuse to give God is the very thing God demands from you.

What you refuse to give God is the very thing God demands from you.

Our problem today is that people try to grow spiritually using their intellectual strength. They're looking for the programs of man to deliver what can be given only by God. They think that through their natural minds they can peer into the spiritual realm. What they find by natural methods are only natural things.

Spiritual freedom is where you have nothing left to lose. "Now, the 'Lord' I'm referring to is the Holy Spirit, and wherever he is Lord, there is freedom" (2 Corinthians 3:17).

The evidence of a life that has surrendered all is a life that has nothing left to lose.

Nobody can touch the life of a believer fully given over to God. The evidence of a life that has surrendered all is a life that has nothing left to lose.

The Lord Jesus taught, "Whoever of you does not forsake all that he has cannot be My disciple" (Luke 14:33). *This is not a question of salvation, but of consecration. When Jesus is the only thing you cannot live without, that is where the life of a disciple begins.*

A life sacrificed to God is a life set free from the tyranny of you.

Your spiritual life grows to the degree the natural life is crucified.

Child of God, so long as you try to grow spiritually using natural methods, you will fail. God is looking for humble believers who recognize their complete inability to do anything of themselves. You must become nothing for Him to be your everything. So long as one ounce of your natural strength is being used to grow in the Spirit, you're only getting in the way.

People think it takes a strong will to walk the higher life. They are wrong. A strong will is an obstacle to growing spiritually.

The greatest hindrance in your spiritual life with God is your efforts to do things through your own natural strength. It is when you kneel lower before Him that He reigns higher over you.

Child of God, if you really want to change, then let Him do the work. Stop agonizing over your failures, and just yield yourself to Him. God knows you can't do it. That's why He sent His Son to save you and His Holy Spirit to empower you. And yet there you are trying, again and again. Stop sobbing over your failures and let Him have His victory in you.

Victory over sin comes only when the Lord Jesus has victory over you. His victory over you comes only when you surrender to Him. If you are struggling with sin, then you are not surrendering.

Yielding produces; yielding allows. No fruit grows unless there is first a yielding over from the ground from which it must come. "The land shall yield its produce, and the trees of the field shall yield their fruit" (Leviticus 26:4).

Stop sobbing over your failures and let Him have His victory in you.

The shocking truth in the life of a believer is when they discover that the sacrifice the Lord requires is their very life. The blessed truth is when the believer discovers that they gain the life of Christ.

It's wonderful when a believer's life is so yielded that the Holy Spirit can move within the believer without any hindrance—where the man or woman has relinquished their rights over to God, and the Spirit of God has moved in and is dwelling with all the riches of heaven. In our natural selves, we think that when we yield we lose. But in the kingdom, when we yield we gain.

To be filled by the Spirit of God, it doesn't take a smart person or a strong person, but a willing person. When you believe that God can fill you, and you yield yourself so that He can, there will be a change in your life like no other. Everything in heaven is ready for you—but are you ready for everything that will come from heaven? To be ready, the only thing you must do is to be yielded. Be yielded.

In the kingdom, when we yield we gain.

A Prayer for Yielding to the Holy Spirit

- *Father God, help me to simply kneel down before You and humbly ask for Your help. Help me to be yielded to You in every area of my life.*

- *Lord Jesus, thank you for modeling a life of yielding to the Father so that I can learn from You the way in which I should live. Help me to have Your life reigning in me by the power of the Holy Spirit.*

- *Holy Spirit, I pray that You would guide me to live a life that's more and more like Jesus. Show me how to yield my life one area at a time to the Lord Jesus, so that His life reigns totally over me.*

Spiritual Guide

- Pray to relinquish rights over your life to God. Start small and give to Him one parcel of your life at a time. Keep going until there's no remaining parcel that you can stand on and call "mine." Resist the urge to take back control. "Whatever work you do, put yourself into it, as those who are serving not merely other people, but the Lord. Remember that as your reward, you will receive the inheritance from the Lord. You are slaving for the Lord, for the Messiah" (Colossians 3:23-24 CJB).

- Practice your humility before men so that you can be humble before God. We must learn to humble ourselves to those whom God has placed in authority over us. If submitting to others offends you, your old nature still remains. We're to be "giving thanks always for all things to God the Father in the name of our Lord Jesus Christ, submitting to one another in the fear of God" (Ephesians 5:20-21).

* Declare in writing those things you're yielding to God. Deed over to Him those areas of your life that still belong to you. Our life in Christ is not supposed to be just in church, but Christ in us. "Then He said to them all, 'If anyone desires to come after Me, let him deny himself, and take up his cross daily, and follow Me'" (Luke 9:23).

21 Word of Knowledge

To hear the Holy Spirit, you must be willing to wait until He speaks to you.

"For to one is given ...the word of knowledge" (1 Corinthians 12:8).

The prison ministry is a ministry of inconvenience, as most ministries are. It's also a ministry where His servants are blessed more than they're a blessing. It was my grandest privilege to minister alongside some of the most anointed servants of God I've ever known in the men's and women's prisons where I served. Many of these mighty servants were prisoners serving time there. I've been most blessed to have some of them continue to minister and encourage me after they were released. I think God can do more in the life of a person who has been crushed, because it's from there that He puts them back together as He has always planned for them to be.

One time, on my way in to preach a service, a correctional officer stopped me at one of the several checkpoints. He asked to pray for me before the service. Another officer at another checkpoint I went through wanted a copy of my sermon to read while I went inside to preach to the men, so that afterward he and I could speak about it. These officers need so much prayer, since they risk their lives to keep us safe. We should pray much for their safety and their salvation.

A few years ago, I preached at a service in a prison where I'd served in ministry for many years. It's a great privilege to serve the Lord. The prison chapel at this higher security complex was a chapel in a cell that held about eighteen inmates. The officers would bring the prisoners in and lock them into that area with me. I loved serving these men. I believe that God can change them, and I wanted to make sure they knew He loves them.

This was a prison chapel where every week we would get a new group of men. This prison was a holding area until they were sent to the long-term prisons where they would serve their term. For some of them, this would be their first time in a church. For others, it might be their last. Consider that as you speak to some people, you might be the only person through whom God might reach them.

Never squander a divine encounter. If the Lord sees fit to put somebody in front of you, be ready to minister to them. "Preach the word! Be ready in season and out of season" (2 Timothy 4:2).

Your ministry is located wherever you are.

Your ministry is located wherever you are.

Your ministry is always in the present tense.

Your mission field is the place where you are standing.

I sat in the back of the chapel, praying while the men were brought in. How much more we could accomplish by simply praying to the One who can achieve so much more than we ever could accomplish in our own power. How much time we waste using up our own energy instead of tapping into His.

After the men sat down, I saw one man from the back who I knew would be saved that day. It was an instant knowing, as if the Lord had spoken it aloud, yet it was just placed in my thoughts. But I knew it was from the Lord. The more we know the Lord, the more we know all that comes from Him. If you want to hear a word into you, you must first have lived your life in the Word.

I had this "knowing" of who would be saved many times before, more than I can count. It's a precious word of knowledge from the Lord, a knowing of what would be. "For to one is given the ...word of knowledge through the same Spirit" (1 Corinthians 12:8).

God is not limited by the imagination of man.

Never limit what the Holy Spirit may do based on your limited understanding.

Never doubt all that the Lord can show you. "Now the LORD gave me knowledge of it, and I know it; for You showed me their doings" (Jeremiah 11:18).

The man I saw who would be saved was a particularly rough-looking man with tattoos all over his body and head. I hadn't seen his face, since I saw him only from behind after I was done praying in the back of the chapel. On the back of his head was a large Nazi swastika.

In my natural self, I look at some people and I think they could never be saved. But there was a time when people said the same thing about me. Don't ever doubt what the Lord can do. This man I saw looked so evil, but I knew what God had shown me, and I personally know what God can do. I want you to know that God can take the most vile man or woman there is and make that person a saint for the kingdom.

Learn to look through your spiritual eyes. Friends, whatever we see on the outside, the Lord can have us look right through it to see what's on the inside. "So God created man in His own image; in the image of God He created him; male and female He created them" (Genesis 1:27).

Never judge a book by its cover, but by its author. God is the author of His children.

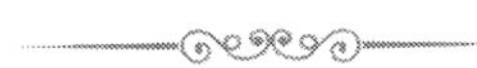

Never judge a book by its cover, but by its author. God is the author of His children.

I spoke a short, uneventful message and then gave an altar call. We don't need a show to save souls—we need the Holy Spirit. We don't need more words of man to move a man, but a word from the Lord that might change him.

So I prayed in the Spirit for anyone who was ready to be saved by the blood of Christ to come up to the front. We need to get people to move, not just sit in their seats. Right off, a man stood up and came to the front. It was not the man the Lord had shown to me. So I kept praying. Praying is good. Persevering in prayer is better.

I prayed that the men wouldn't let the devil hold them down in their seats, and that they would just stand up. Right then, two more men stood up. But still not the one I was expecting.

The work of the Lord is never easy, and He never operates by our estimation of how things should go. But just keep serving anyway.

Stop expecting that ministry would be easy. God can do the best work through the worst circumstances, and we need to trust Him in the process.

God can do the best work through the worst circumstances, and we need to trust Him in the process.

One of the greatest hindrances in serving God is your false idea that He is going to make it easy for you. He will always be with you—that is enough.

I just kept praying. I knew what the Lord had shown to me—the exact man who would be saved. The Lord has never failed me. Child of God, He will never fail you. If He gives you a word, that word will come to pass. "So shall My word be that goes forth from My mouth; It shall not return to Me void, but it shall accomplish what I please, and it shall prosper in the thing for which I sent it" (Isaiah 55:11).

So I prayed and I prayed, and they kept standing, and they kept coming forward—but not yet the man I expected.

Only three men in that chapel were still sitting. Some big men were standing up front, so I had to stand tip-toed to look over their shoulders at the man I knew would get saved that day. Right when I looked at him, he stood up and came forward. Sometimes we need to look a man or woman in the eye to stir up their soul.

All but two of the men at that service came to the altar to be saved that day. Before praying a prayer of salvation, I asked everybody, "Who is here for the very first time getting saved?" We have many in the ministry who are repeats at the altar, backsliders who keep coming back to the altar. The Lord is always waiting for those who'll return to Him. I always pray for those who are recommitting, but I want to pray differently for a man or woman getting saved for the first time.

On this day, only one of the men standing was there to be saved for the first time. He was the last man to stand up. It was the swastika-marked man that the Lord had shown me before the service had begun. It was the one who in the natural nobody would think could be saved. His name was Jason, and on that day in the chapel there on Bravo yard, he got saved!

If you want to hear a word from the Holy Spirit, you need to be in a place of holiness. Confess your sin that you would be cleansed. The washing always precedes the anointing.

If you want to be used by God, you have to be willing to give up the right to yourself.

If you want to be used by God, you have to be willing to give up the right to yourself.

Never think you need to be anything in yourself. In fact, you cannot be anything in yourself to be used of God. You are only the utensil through which He might pour out His power onto a fallen world.

Pray that you would hear the Holy Spirit. Then be still and listen. "However, when He, the Spirit of truth, has come, He will guide you into all truth; for He will not speak on His own authority, but whatever He hears He will speak; and He will tell you things to come" (John 16:13).

When you offer an altar call, you don't have to know who will get saved. And even if nobody comes up, the Lord is still doing a work. Often, all you're doing is preparing the heart of a man or woman for another day. So be that one who prepares. It doesn't matter how many we introduce to the Lord, but how many we influence to the Lord along the way. It's not a competition but a commission.

And don't think you need to be in a church or have an altar to do an altar call. When you witness to a person, wherever you are, and they've heard the gospel, give them the chance to receive Christ into their lives. Child of God, we need more than a one-time surrender at an altar call; we need to build men and women into disciples. So encourage them to press in for something more.

After the altar call, I spent time prophesying over each man who came up. I remember two men in particular, and what I spoke to them. They were both very muscular and looked like what you would expect a gang member to look like. I heard a word for the first man, and I told him that he needed to stop running from the Lord. He told me he wasn't running. I asked him to pray about it. I also heard a word for the second man, and I told him that even though he looked so tough on the outside, he had a tender heart. Immediately he burst into tears and started weeping. After this the officers came and took the men back to their cells.

A few weeks later, I was in a different prison at a service. I saw the man I'd prophesied over about his tender heart. It was a joy to see him coming to church at this other prison. He told me he'd given his life to Christ. We spoke about his friend who I'd prophesied over and who was running from the Lord. He confirmed that this was true and that his friend knew it. The Lord blesses us with confirmations so that we gain in our confidence that we're hearing Him with clarity. When we're led by the Holy Spirit, and we're obedient to follow Him, we'll never go the wrong way.

Don't squander an opportunity, and don't try to do more than what He gives you.

I've never seen either of those two men again. When we're used of God, it's often for only a moment in the lives of those He puts in front of us. Don't squander an opportunity, and don't try to do more than what He gives you.

A Prayer to Gain a Word of Knowledge from the Holy Spirit

* *Father God, it doesn't matter how many I reach as I serve You; what matters is only that I minister to that one person You've appointed me to serve in that moment. Help me to serve You in obscurity and humility.*

* *Lord Jesus, I pray for those in prisons across this world, that You will send Your servants to minister to them, so that these prisoners may find redemption and hope in You alone.*

* *Holy Spirit, teach me to hear Your voice so that I do only as You would have me do. Help me to receive anything from You in humility, so that You have no hindrance in me.*

Spiritual Guide

- Never pretend with your faith, because the Lord is bringing a day when everything will be revealed. "For there is nothing covered that will not be revealed, nor hidden that will not be known" (Luke 12:2).

- Do not seek the gifts that you could then serve. Rather, seek for God to give you everything you need in the midst of your serving. Jesus taught us, "If anyone desires to be first, he shall be last of all and servant of all" (Mark 9:35).

- See that you judge no one, and then your life will be a blessing to many. Jesus taught, "Judge not, and you shall not be judged. Condemn not, and you shall not be condemned. Forgive, and you will be forgiven" (Luke 6:37).

22 Weight of Glory

The weight of glory cannot be measured on the scales of man.

Our "affliction...is working for us a far more exceeding and eternal weight of glory" (2 Corinthians 4:17).

When the presence of God increases, His glory becomes unbearable to our frail human frame. When Moses prayed that he might see God, he had to be hidden by a rock, and he saw only the passing presence of God, since he wouldn't have been able to bear anything more. "So it shall be, while My glory passes by, that I will put you in the cleft of the rock, and will cover you with My hand while I pass by" (Exodus 33:22).

When King Solomon opened up the temple in Jerusalem for the first time, the presence of the glory of God was so great in that temple that nobody was able to enter it. "When Solomon had finished praying, fire came down from heaven and consumed the burnt offering and the sacrifices; and the glory of the LORD filled the temple. And the priests could not enter the house of the LORD, because the glory of the LORD had filled the LORD's house" (2 Chronicles 7:1-2).

The glory of the Lord is as great and mighty today as it was for Moses and as it was for Solomon. Our God has eternal strength, and His glory will never diminish. Just look to the stars, for they proclaim His glory. "The heavens declare the glory of God" (Psalm 19:1).

His glory can be revealed on earth as we surrender before Him. Moses and Solomon were mere human beings like you and me. If we would dare to surrender ourselves to God, to yield ourselves unto His glory, then He will show up in ways we never imagined, and we'll be forever touched by a God whose glory is forever.

E.M. Bounds was born in 1835 and was an anointed pastor who spoke much on prayer. In his writings, Bounds tells about an all-night prayer meeting in England held long before his time, on December 31, 1738. In attendance were some mighty men of God, including John Wesley and George Whitfield, two of the mightiest Spirit-filled Christian leaders of that day. Bounds quotes Wesley's account from that night: "About three o'clock in the morning, as we were continuing instant in prayer, the power of God came mightily upon us, so that many cried out for exceeding joy, and many fell to the ground."

There is so much power and majesty in the glory of the Lord, that mere mortals cannot remain standing and the hearts of men tremble before all they see. We read about the power of God in Scripture and how His glory affects people. "The priests could not stand to minister because of the cloud, for the glory of the LORD filled the house of God" (2 Chronicles 5:14 NASB).

You know that the weight of glory has filled the house of God when nobody can remain standing.

Several years ago, I went to a prayer meeting held at a home church. There was such a move of the Holy Spirit that you could literally feel it in the air. There was a man there who was praying over people. As he prayed, many would become so filled with the glory of the Lord that they would fall to the ground.

I know this falling isn't always real, and I can sense when it is and when it isn't. Sometimes it's faked or fawned, or not even of the Holy Spirit. But when it's of God, there's such a presence of the glory that one simply cannot remain standing anymore. We must beware of what's wrong, but not discount what is of God. That was the error of the Pharisees, who stood on the Word but didn't see the Son of God when He was standing right before them. Always discern, but remain open to a movement of God.

You know that the weight of glory has filled the house of God when nobody can remain standing.

Only those who never experience the power of the Holy Spirit can argue against it. And argue they will, so they can justify their own lack.

Never try to convince someone who is bent on not believing. You can never prove by sight to those who are blind, nor by sound to those that are deaf.

"Jesus said to her, 'Did I not say to you that if you would believe you would see the glory of God?'" (John 11:40). Imagine your life "if you would believe."

Imagine your life "if you would believe."

I've experienced this weight of glory many times, but on this night I was determined to stay on the edge by myself. I was all set to preach two services the next morning in prison, but I felt so alone and separated from the Father. I didn't feel worthy to be that near to the Lord on this night. Usually if I sit to the side, it's there that I remain. There are usually so many who need prayer that nobody would ever bother with someone who does not. I just wanted to be by myself in prayer.

But the man of God saw me and had me stand up with him. He said that he saw a dark cloud that was all around me. I felt the same thing. I'd been feeling as though I was being spiritually attacked as never before. There were so many demons in the prisons where I was ministering. I was going up against so much darkness. May we always be ready to receive help from our brothers and sisters in Christ as we face the battles in ministry. Always remember that sometimes we must go up on the mountain to see the glory, so then we can be prepared to walk in the darkness in the valley below. We aren't called to live on the mountain, but sometimes we need to go there.

Sometimes we must go up on the mountain to see the glory, so then we can be prepared to walk in the darkness in the valley below.

To go from glory to glory, you cannot remain as you are.

What was good enough before will not be enough for what He has for you. "But we all...are being transformed into the same image from glory to glory, just as by the Spirit of the Lord" (2 Corinthians 3:18).

An increase from glory to glory comes only by the Spirit of the Lord.

The Lord Jesus will draw you up to the next level just as soon as you are obedient to the level where you are now. "We are being changed into His very image, from one degree of glory to the next, by Adonai the Spirit." (2 Corinthians 3:18 CJB). *Glory increases upon glory.*

When the man of God prayed over me, without so much as touching me, I fell instantly to the ground—not of my own power nor by the power of man. I was laid out on my back, and I felt the weight of glory upon me. I felt the Holy Spirit holding me down and doing a new thing in me. It was as if there was an intense sanctification going on to a

The Lord Jesus will draw you up to the next level just as soon as you are obedient to the level where you are now.

degree I'd never experienced. Whatever darkness had been around me, there was only light that could remain.

Most times the Lord will send someone to minister to us in our need. But sometimes it will be the Holy Spirit, the Comforter, who will come upon you and bring to you what no human ever could. The comfort from heaven cannot be compared to what we receive from people on earth. The intentions of man are sometimes good, but a move of God is always better.

I don't know how long I was like this, laid out on the ground. I literally felt a weight so heavy upon me that I couldn't get up on my own strength. It was the most beautiful thing ever. It was as if I was held in the grip of God, pinned down by the Holy Spirit while He did a work inside me. When I finally got up, I was so overwhelmed that I had to go outside where I could weep by myself. Nobody gets past the Holy Spirit without tears.

There is a greater glory in the Spirit than in the stone. "But if the ministry of death, written and engraved on stones, was glorious, so that the children of Israel could not look steadily at the face of Moses because of the glory of his countenance, which glory was passing away, how will the ministry of the Spirit not be more glorious?" (2 Corinthians 3:7-8).

Do not seek the wisdom of man to solve the mysteries of God. "To them God willed to make known what are the riches of the glory of this mystery among the Gentiles: which is Christ in you, the hope of glory" (Colossians 1:27).

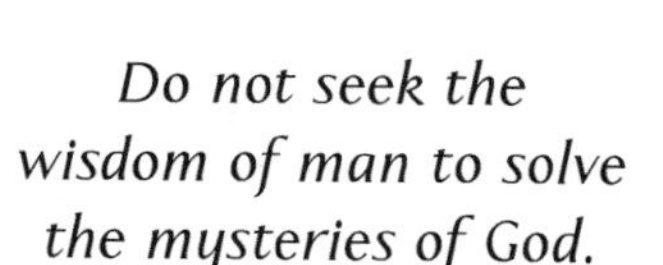

Do not seek the wisdom of man to solve the mysteries of God.

Be filled with the Holy Spirit so that you are forever content, yet never be satisfied to remain as you are.

Oh, how I pray that the weight of His glory would bring you to your knees.

Child of God, don't ever stop growing spiritually. Don't let your natural understanding of things block the spiritual understanding that only the Holy Spirit can teach you. Don't ever think our supernatural God is limited by the natural in which we live. Stay grounded in the Word, and keep reaching for the things of heaven.

Stay grounded in the Word, and keep reaching for the things of heaven.

Seek to experience the spiritual life you long for. You were meant for something more. There's so much more. Don't believe the spiritually dry teachers. There's a richness of glory available to you, which is Christ in you. There's a power of the Holy Spirit so rich and so full, if you would only pray for it.

The weight of glory comes only with the presence of God. It happened thousands of years ago at the opening of Solomon's temple. It happened some three hundred years ago at a little home in England, with John Wesley and George. Child of God, I want you to know that God is waiting for that man or woman who will dare to pray into the greater presence of God in their life today.

What is greater than falling in the Spirit is getting back up and walking in the Spirit. Don't chase the experiences, rather let the experiences change you. It takes only a single touch from God for your life to be changed forever. Better to be changed by a single touch than to chase a thousand touches and remain as you are after each one.

Don't chase the experiences, rather let the experiences change you.

Don't worship the experience more than the God who gave it to you. Be willing to get nothing, and perhaps in your submission He will give you something. We'll spend eternity trying to remain standing in His presence. Be content that He usually allows you to remain standing for now.

A Prayer for Experiencing the Weight of His Glory

* *Father God, help me to not be seeking experiences from You more than I'm seeking You. Help me to want only to draw nearer to You, knowing that in You I'll have everything I need.*

* *Lord Jesus, let me not seek signs, but be a witness for the power of Your blood to save me and anyone else willing to accept You. Help me to be satisfied in You alone.*

* *Holy Spirit, come upon me only to the degree that I remain humble and devoted to serving the Father in humility and truth. Display the life of Jesus through me.*

Spiritual Guide

* Study the Word deeper, from cover to cover. Never be satisfied with what you know. "Yahweh [The LORD] advises those who fear Him. He reveals to them the intent of His promise." (Psalm 25:14 NOG).

* Seek for others with whom you can pray. A principle of unity is that we can do more with others than we can do alone. "For where two or three are gathered together in My name, I am there in the midst of them" (Matthew 18:20).

* Seek to live in a deeper humility with those around you. Stay as low as you can so there's less distance by which you might fall. "For I say, through the grace given to me, to everyone who is among you, not to think of himself more highly than he ought to think, but to think soberly, as God has dealt to each one a measure of faith" (Romans 12:3).

23 Living the Revelation Life

Revelation does not come by the efforts of man, but by the power of God.

"For I neither received it from man, nor was I taught it, but it came through the revelation of Jesus Christ" (Galatians 1:12).

There's a level in your faith that you can reach where the Holy Spirit will bring you revelations of truth. Jesus promised that the Holy Spirit would teach us all things, and those things aren't yet revealed to us until the Holy Spirit helps us see them. Jesus promised us, "The Helper, the Holy Spirit, whom the Father will send in My name, He will teach you all things" (John 14:26).

This promise is the promise of revelation. When we're taught something, it's revealed to us. The Holy Spirit will reveal to us and teach us things we couldn't know in any other way. You can study for all your life, but apart from the Holy Spirit you'll be able to see only as far as your natural eyes can get you.

Our first and most important source of truth in this day is the Word of God. We need the Spirit of God to help us understand the depths in the Word of God—not only the literary or historical depths, but the spiritual depths. Men will read stacks of the commentaries of man, and we can learn much from these books. But what we truly need is the greatest commentator there is, the Holy Spirit.

Our first and most important source of truth in this day is the Word of God.

The revelation life is one in which the man or woman of God is led and taught by the Holy Spirit—where the Holy Spirit is pouring into the believer revelations of truth that they can get in no other way. The first and greatest revelation is knowing Jesus—not just knowing about Him, but knowing Him personally. Some revelation is known by many, but it's revelatory in your life when it becomes known to you. Some revelation is new, but it's always built upon the old. Truth can never change, but only be expounded upon.

There's no secret to living the revelation life other than confessing Jesus as Lord and being led and taught by the Holy Spirit. I see some who parade their life before men to be noticed, and they'll get their due reward in the end. Be sure that if it's something truly of God, it will not promote the person on whom it rests. If Jesus washed the feet of His disciples, how much lower should we be?

Revelation never comes by striving but by abiding, where the believer is abiding in the presence of Christ Jesus. If you want to learn more from the Holy Spirit, you must stay in the presence of Jesus. Whenever you read the Word of God, pray that the Holy Spirit will reveal the truths of God through His Word to you.

You cannot reach the depths of God using the natural tools of man. Knowledge comes through study, but revelation comes only from God.

You cannot take revelation that only He can give. The apostle Paul prayed "that the God of our Lord Jesus Christ, the Father of glory, may give to you the spirit of wisdom and revelation in the knowledge of Him, the eyes of your understanding being enlightened" (Ephesians 1:17-18).

Knowledge of the world is attained. Knowledge of the Lord is received. Pray for the Holy Spirit to teach you truths that only He can understand, and that only He is qualified to teach you.

Knowledge of the world is attained. Knowledge of the Lord is received.

The barrier to revelation is insisting on gaining it yourself.

Revelation is a mystery solved and the truth uncovered. As Paul wrote, "By revelation He made known to me the mystery" (Ephesians 3:3).

Often the arguments we have with others are not about the truth itself, but about the degree to which the truth has been revealed to each one of us. Never argue with another person over a revelation that's not yet revealed into that person's heart.

Be understanding when others haven't received the revelations you have, and be humble to receive corrections or deeper revelations from another.

To gain worldly wisdom requires much effort. To gain heavenly wisdom requires much submission.

To gain worldly wisdom requires much effort. To gain heavenly wisdom requires much submission.

Revelation requires sight to see the revealed. You can see revelation only with your spiritual eyes open. Your natural vision is a hindrance to spiritual truths.

Revelation is being shown the truth that is often hidden in plain sight. You don't need to search afar to discover more truth; just pray that the Holy Spirit would reveal all that is before you.

The great test we must apply as we seek revelation from God is what our motives are. All of us are susceptible to our pride, wanting to be something more than we are. When we gain revelation, we must realize that it's never by anything we can be proud of, but only by what we can be humbled by. God is so gracious to share a hidden truth for fools like us to see.

The revelation life is not for the proud, for they want to take credit for everything they know. The Lord will not entrust the riches of spiritual truth to the proud, for they wouldn't treat it as the holy, reverent, and blessed truth from heaven that it is. Revelations are treasures.

We should also be cautious about whom we share revelations with, since many would simply not receive them, and might even become hateful toward us for sharing. This is why Jesus taught us this truth, "Do not give what is holy to the dogs; nor cast your pearls before swine, lest they trample them under their feet, and turn and tear you in pieces" (Matthew 7:6). Revelations from the Holy Spirit are the greatest pearls, so give those pearls only to those who would see them as the treasures they are.

Revelation is not always seeing something new, but having something revealed that was there all along. It is not that God has hidden the truth, but only that we are blind to see it, deaf to hear it, and with a heart that cannot understand it. "Yet the LORD has not given you a heart to perceive and eyes to see and ears to hear, to this very day" (Deuteronomy 29:4).

Spiritual senses are never attained, only received. It is never a matter of trying harder but yielding more.

Revelation never changes a truth of God, but only expounds upon what has already been given.

> *Revelation never changes a truth of God, but only expounds upon what has already been given.*

The more we understand, the more we will trust in Him. The more we trust in Him, the more He will reveal. "The secret of the LORD is with those who fear Him, and He will show them His covenant" (Psalm 25:14).

Sometimes we think revelation is only about seeing all that might happen in the future. Yet the prophets of old would rarely see a revelation come to pass. Isaiah had many revelations on the life of Christ, but his life was ended some seven hundred years before Christ was even born. If you read the prophetic books, you will find that many of the revelations were revealing only the truth of what was happening in that day.

Beware of the fortune tellers in our day who masquerade as prophets and tell men what they want to hear—who preach revelations for profit and give a word to men that they might be made the richer. The Lord will deal with them soon enough. "The prophets prophesy falsely, and the priests rule by their own power; and My people love to have it so. But what will you do in the end?" (Jeremiah 5:31).

Also, don't be afraid of prophets, but be discerning. Jesus taught us, "Beware of false prophets, who come to you in sheep's clothing, but inwardly they are ravenous wolves. You will know them by their fruits" (Matthew 7:15-16). Jesus cautions us about false prophets, which means that there are true prophets.

And don't think that revelations are only for prophets. Jesus promised that the Holy Spirit would teach us all things. Revelatory teaching from the Holy Spirit is meant for all of us, since the Spirit was poured out onto anyone who would receive Him.

Living the Revelation Life

The Word revealed, revives. "Where there is no revelation, the people cast off restraint; but happy is he who keeps the law" (Proverbs 29:18).

Revelation is not meant to elevate us, but to change us. If revelation doesn't change you, what's the point? Pray that the Lord will reveal something in you that needs to change this day.

Revelation is not meant to elevate us, but to change us.

Intellectualism is often the obstacle to spiritual understanding.

Revelation cannot be found through the wisdom of man. The wisdom of man is foolishness to God, and the wisdom of God is foolishness to man.

Those who teach and preach on the Word of God have a great responsibility. Nobody is able to do it rightly on their own power. We need to press in that the Holy Spirit would reveal to us all that we're to teach. And we must do so soberly, knowing the stricter judgment that awaits us. "My brethren, let not many of you become teachers, knowing that we shall receive a stricter judgment" (James 3:1).

If you're a preacher or teacher of the Word, I pray that His Spirit will be upon you. How much we need in our day men and women filled with the Holy Spirit, centered on the life of Christ, and serving the Father in all humility. Don't fear walking in revelation, but fear walking without it.

Preaching Revelation

The greatest revelation you can preach is Jesus Christ. "The Revelation of Jesus Christ, which God gave Him to show His servants" (Revelation 1:1).

You cannot preach revelation to those in darkness, because they cannot yet see. Instead, preach light, that they would step into it.

Revelation attracts the most critics, thus exposing them. Be led by the Holy Spirit, not critics.

Don't try to explain more so that your preaching is safer, but reveal more so that your teaching is more effective.

You will never satisfy the arguments in the natural when the subject requires spiritual understanding. "We don't speak about these things using teachings that are based on intellectual arguments like people do. Instead, we use the Spirit's teachings. We explain spiritual things to those who have the Spirit. A person who isn't spiritual doesn't accept the teachings of God's Spirit. He thinks they're nonsense. He can't understand them because a person must be spiritual to evaluate them." (1 Corinthians 2:13-14 NOG).

Don't try to explain more so that your preaching is safer, but reveal more so that your teaching is more effective.

The more natural you put in your message, the less spiritual will remain.

In our greatest struggles, God leads us on a path where His truth can flow through us onto others. Live the lesson so that you can then teach it.

Pray that you would grow in your spiritual life. Pray that you would begin to walk in greater revelations. Pray that as you read the Word of God, the Living Word, it will come alive in you. This is never going to happen by your qualifications, but only through your surrender and His great power.

A Prayer for Living the Revelation Life

* *Father God, help me to discover new truths in Your Word so that my life is changed and I become a sweet aroma to You.*

* *Lord Jesus, help me, so that Your life is revealed in me. Help me gain new and wonderful revelations about the truths You taught and lived.*

* *Holy Spirit, help me to be moved by You, and teach me new and fresh revelations so that I not only learn these new things, but also live them, so that I'm a living epistle for Christ.*

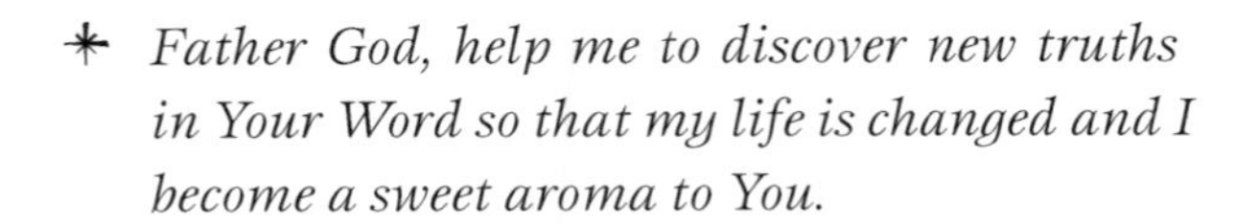

Spiritual Guide

* Pray that the Lord will show you new things. There is so much more for you to learn. It will take eternity to discover all the truths in God's Word. "Call to Me, and I will answer you, and show you great and mighty things, which you do not know" (Jeremiah 33:3).

* Don't fear men when sharing revelations, but fear God. "But as we have been approved by God to be entrusted with the gospel, even so we speak, not as pleasing men, but God who tests our hearts" (1 Thessalonians 2:4).

* Seek revelation in the Word of God to live it, not just to know it. "But be doers of the word, and not hearers only, deceiving yourselves" (James 1:22).

24 Preaching in the Holy Spirit

The problem with most sermons is that they're born out of the tomb of men's offices and not from the life of the Holy Spirit within.

"And my speech and my preaching were not with persuasive words of *human* wisdom, but in demonstration of the Spirit and of power" (1 Corinthians 2:4).

I look back to when I first started preaching in prisons, and I can see that the messages were well-intentioned, studied, prepared, organized, and based on the Word of God. But when I was preparing and preaching these messages, I was doing them in my own power. It's by the grace of God that no recording devices were allowed in prison, so that I don't have to listen even for one minute to one of these earlier messages of mine. I've looked at some of what I'd written for them, and I can see the zealousness in my faith but the lack of anything from the Holy Spirit.

The weakest messages are written by the strongest minds.

The weakest messages are written by the strongest minds.

If the Holy Spirit is your teacher, then why are you learning only from the minds of man?

I can always tell when a message has no Holy Spirit by how much of man I find in it.

Some teachers spend more time building PowerPoints than they do praying. Technology cannot replace the Holy Spirit, and often just gets in the way.

My greatest hope is that you would lean into a greater moving of the Holy Spirit in however you're teaching or preaching to others. Whether your audience is a large group or a single soul, and whether young or old, my prayer is that the Spirit of God will move within you as you minister to whoever He has placed in your path. Be sure that your ministry is to whomever the Lord sets before you.

We think we need to add to what God has, but it is the other way around.

If you worry about being rejected by men, you cannot be used much by God.

The greatest hindrance in your ministry is you. The greatest obstacle to your ministry is falling short at the limit of you.

Ministry is not for only the few but for all. Ministry is not something you do, but the life you live. Ministry isn't a part of your life; it *is* your life. There are no spectators needed in the fields, but only laborers. God has ordained for some to be reached by you, and my prayer is that you would let Him help you in the process. Every one of us is uniquely designed with our own experiences so that we can reach some who nobody else can. But we need the power of the Holy Spirit within us so that we might do it rightly.

We often have more gimmicks in our churches than we have the Holy Spirit, and we wonder why people's lives are not being changed. Gimmicks will entertain, but it takes the Holy Spirit to transform the person.

Ministry isn't a part of your life; it is your life.

The more you read from your notes, the less He can speak through you. "Do not worry about how or what you should answer, or what you should say. For the Holy Spirit will teach you in that very hour what you ought to say" (Luke 12:11-12).

Sometimes you need to put your notes down and let the Holy Spirit preach through you.

I was most blessed to be mentored for many years by Dr. Donald Warrick, the State Prison Chaplain at a prison I ministered at. It was while serving in Dr. Warrick's church that I first saw the power of God and the movement of the Holy Spirit.

I remember one Sunday watching Dr. Warrick preach in the Spirit. He'd invited me to be with him in his church that he pastored in the prison. We went to the first prison yard, and I saw him get up to preach. I was sitting right next to the small podium where he was going to preach from. He had no outline or notes. He had no PowerPoint presentation, and no technology to display anything. He quietly opened his Bible, went to a verse, and then I saw the Spirit fall upon him.

It was is if he became a different man. "Then the Spirit of the Lord will come upon you, and you will prophesy with them and be turned into another man" (1 Samuel 10:6). Dr. Warrick became filled with the power of the Holy Ghost upon him, and he preached a message in a way I'd never heard before. It was a message that reached in and stirred up my spirit. After the message, he came back and sat next to me, and he returned to the person he was before.

Later that afternoon, we went to a separate prison yard with a different chapel. Again, I sat next to him as he stepped up to the podium. Like before, he stepped up to the podium and quietly opened his Bible, going to the same verse as the first service. Then I saw the Spirit of God fall upon him as before. I was waiting to hear the same message I heard at the first service. But though the verse was the same, the entire message was different, and was a further revelation of the truth in the verse from which he was preaching.

It was after this that I set out to change how I might preach. Not by my abilities, but by God's abilities. Not by my preparation of the message, but by the surrendering of myself. How much we need our preachers and our teachers to be men and women of God, surrendered to God, used of God, filled of God, to the glory of God.

The same Holy Spirit who filled the apostle Peter fills you.

The same Holy Spirit who filled the apostle Peter fills you. Stop thinking God cannot do great things through you, and just let Him.

You can always tell a preacher who does not have the Holy Spirit as his teacher, because all his inspiration comes from the commentaries of man.

Our problem is that we have more words from man than from the Lord in our services.

My greatest hope is that we will have more teachers and preachers filled by the Holy Spirit as they're being used as instruments for the kingdom of God. My prayer is that we will have not only signs and wonders in our churches, but a Spirit-filled word that echoes into the spirit of the believers. I'm convinced we can do more by one word from the Holy Spirit than a stack of books with the wisdom of man. Pray for your pastors. Pray for your teachers. Pray for your church to be pliable in the hands of God. Pray for the Holy Spirit to be welcome in your church.

Several years ago, we had a summer series of Sunday night services at an outside church I was attending. I was most blessed to be on the prayer team that spent the entire service in the back room praying for the pastor and the people to be moved by the Spirit of God. Sometimes we would pray a prophetic word identifying the particular situation with a person in the service and what they needed prayer for. After the service, we would go out and offer prayer, and be so blessed to meet the very person with the exact problem about which we'd been prophetically praying about.

Beloved child of God, if you don't see a move of the Spirit at your church right now, be the one who starts it. Pray into all that God would do. Pray believing. God is looking for believers who pray believing.

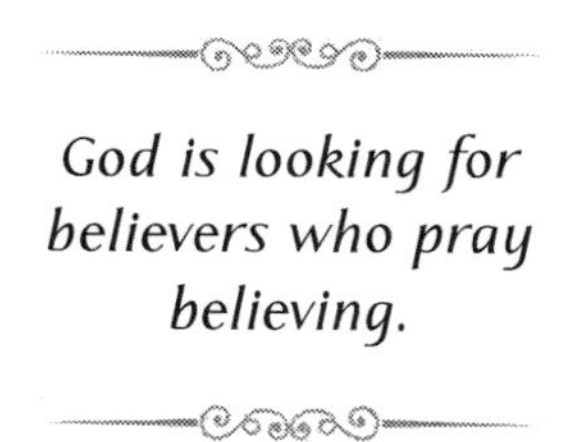
God is looking for
believers who pray
believing.

You cannot force the power of the Holy Spirit from you, because you are not the source. It is only when you surrender in the natural that His supernatural can flow through you.

Prepare as you must, but be willing to let the Holy Spirit interrupt the service at any time.

The main requirement to serving God is being filled by the Holy Spirit; everything else is only to impress man. When the apostles sought out those to serve in the church, their message was, "Seek out from among you seven men of good reputation, full of the Holy Spirit and wisdom, whom we may appoint" (Acts 6:3).

I'll never forget the first time I felt the Spirit of God rest upon me as I was preaching. There's no one who needs more help than I do; my speaking is weak, my presence isn't impressive, and my intellect is lacking. I felt so weak and useless in ministry, afraid to even do an altar call because it would expose the weakness and futility of my preaching. How often we're ministering and thinking that it's by our abilities that the Lord will accomplish His purposes. The Lord's power works through us, and until we get that, we're only in His way.

The best messages ever preached were not written by men.

The best messages ever preached were not written by men.

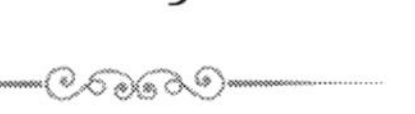

The Lord Jesus said, "He who believes in Me, as the Scripture has said, out of his heart will flow rivers of living water." And John tells us, "He spoke concerning the Spirit, whom those believing in Him would receive" (John 7:38-39). *We have many hearts behind the pulpits, but few rivers.*

If you want to have a move of God, you must get out of His way.

It is good to work for God, but divine to have God work through you. One relies upon yourself, the other entirely upon Him.

I used to worry in my preaching that I might offend some people. Now I worry more that I might offend the Lord. Let us never think we must be popular to be right, since it's often the other way around. In however the Lord is using you, be willing to be moved by Him, and never be moved by man.

The preacher is not there to coddle the people in their sin, but to warn them of the judgment that awaits them. Stop preaching a soft message that leaves people going to hell.

Just because your church is full of people does not mean they're going to heaven. Somebody needs to tell them. Fear the judgment of God more than the judgment of man.

What is more important to you: serving God, or impressing men? You will do more for men when you determine to no longer try to impress them.

Preach the Word, and let the cards fall as they will.

Child of God, fear God, then let Him worry about the people around you. Serve God wherever you are—that is your reasonable service to Him. Seek to be filled by the Holy Spirit, then let Him give you the words you speak.

You can serve Him by His qualifications, not yours.

You can serve Him by His qualifications, not yours.

A Prayer for Preaching in the Holy Spirit

- *Father God, help me to see that what matters is what You think, and that I answer to You and not to man. Let me not use this to avoid the authority You place over me, but to ensure Your authority is higher.*

- *Lord Jesus, help me to preach and teach faithfully, with the ultimate message of Your life crucified. Help me not only to draw people to the altar, but to build them up in their faith once they get there.*

- *Holy Spirit, help me to yield myself over to You, so that You have the right of way to minister through me to whomever the Father places before me, right where they are.*

Spiritual Guide

- Never be satisfied with not being an instrument for God. Wherever you are, and whomever God places in front of you, pray that the Holy Spirit would move through you. “And Jabez called on the God of Israel saying, ‘Oh, that

You would bless me indeed, and enlarge my territory, that Your hand would be with me...'" (1 Chronicles 4:10).

- In however you're called to serve the Lord, test yourself by not preparing by your natural strength. Instead, place your trust in Him. Jesus taught us, "Do not worry beforehand, or premeditate what you will speak. But whatever is given you in that hour, speak that; for it is not you who speak, but the Holy Spirit" (Mark 13:11).

- Learn not to fear when you speak in front of someone. Just trust that the Lord has everything under His perfect sovereign control. "For God has not given us a spirit of fear, but of power and of love and of a sound mind" (2 Timothy 1:7).

Acknowledgments

Mary Balius, my best friend and precious wife. You are my most treasured gift from the Lord. You are the heart of the ministry I walk in and the joy I come home to every night. I love you forever and then some.

My parents, Herbert and Patricia Balius, who have been my model for godly living and the greatest intercessors for my life and for all my work in ministry. Your prayers have moved mountains and your prayers have moved me.

My children and grandchildren, who are such a blessing to me and inspire me to be better than I am. Forever in my heart are your names in the order I was blessed to meet you: Sarah, Trevor, Annie, Duyen, Erik, Emily, and Ellie.

Thomas Womack, for your mastery in editing, for helping me find my voice, and for your guidance to help me navigate the world of book publishing. *http://www.bookox.com/*

Tamara Dever from TLC Book Design, thank you so much for your guidance and wisdom in helping me to produce a book. You are a gift from God. *https://tlcbookdesign.com/*

Monica Thomas from TLC Book Design, for all the wonderful work you did on the cover design and interior layout. Your work is a masterpiece and I am blessed to have met you. *https://tlcbookdesign.com/*

Dana Cobb, for your meticulous proofreading and all your recommendations. I admire your knowledge and skill.

Ilse Kleyn, for the privilege of using the dove from one of your paintings on the cover of this book. I hope many will be blessed by your gift from God. *http://artofkleyn.com/*

I want to thank the many precious souls who have poured into my life and blessed me with their friendship, counsel, and prayers. I could never name everyone here, but your names are written on my heart and spoken in my prayers.

About the Author

Paul Michael Balius was born in Lynwood, California, near Los Angeles, and grew up nearby. He was raised in a Christian home by parents who were forged out of the farmlands of Iowa. Though Paul did not come to faith until later in life, he was surrounded by a godly family throughout his childhood.

When Paul was twenty-three, he was married to his best friend and soulmate, Mary Ann De La Paz. Mary was a believer before Paul, and she saw to it their children went to church every week. Some years later, Paul gave his life to Jesus and then immersed himself for many years in studying all the things of the Lord.

Paul became filled with a passion to serve the Lord. He joined Prison Fellowship Ministries where he served for fourteen years. He ended up teaching and preaching three days a week or more at three different state prisons. While serving in this ministry, he met many mighty believers who walked in the power of the Holy Spirit.

While in the prison ministry, Paul was filled with the Holy Spirit and began to experience the gifts of the Holy Spirit. He was grounded in conservative teachings, and now found himself reaching for the spiritual things of heaven. He discovered that the spiritual promises in the Word were all true.

After fourteen years with Prison Fellowship, the Lord gave Paul a firm calling to step out of the prison ministry and into the ministry of writing. It is now Paul's life mission from God to teach and inspire others to grow in their spiritual life and become all that God has ordained them to be.

Paul and Mary currently reside in Orange, California. It would be a great honor for Paul if you would visit his online ministry.

Ministry website: *https://Hehasyou.org/*
Ministry Facebook: *https://www.facebook.com/Hehasyou/*

Made in United States
Orlando, FL
25 November 2022